THE
Eleven ~~TEN~~ COMMANDMENTS
OF
GOOD TEACHING

Second Edition

THE ~~Ten~~ Eleven COMMANDMENTS OF GOOD TEACHING

Second Edition

Creating Classrooms Where Teachers Can Teach and Students Can Learn

Vickie Gill

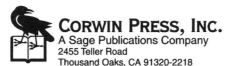

CORWIN PRESS, INC.
A Sage Publications Company
2455 Teller Road
Thousand Oaks, CA 91320-2218
E-mail: order@corwinpress.com
Call: (800) 818-7243 Fax: (800) 4-1-SCHOOL
www.corwinpress.com

For information:

Corwin Press, Inc.
A Sage Publications Company
2455 Teller Road
Thousand Oaks, California 91320
E-mail: order@corwinpress.com

Sage Publications Ltd.
6 Bonhill Street
London EC2A 4PU
United Kingdom

Sage Publications India Pvt. Ltd.
M-32 Market
Greater Kailash I
New Delhi 110 048 India

Printed in the United States of America

Library of Congress Cataloging-in-Publication Data

Gill, Vickie.
    The eleven commandments of good teaching: Creating classrooms where teachers can teach and students can learn / by Vickie Gill.— 2nd ed.
        p. cm.
    Rev. ed. of: The ten commandments of good teaching. c1998.
    ISBN 0-7619-7809-7 (cloth: acid-free paper) — ISBN 0-7619-7810-0 (pbk.: acid-free paper)
    1. Effective teaching. I. Title: 11 commandments of good teaching.
    II. Gill, Vickie. Ten commandments of good teaching. III. Title.
LB1025.3 .G45 2001
371.102—dc21   0-012371

This book is printed on acid-free paper.

01 02 03 04 05 06 07 7 6 5 4 3 2 1

Acquiring Editor:	Rachel Livsey
Corwin Editorial Assistant:	Phyllis Cappello
Production Editor:	Diane S. Foster
Editorial Assistant:	Cindy Bear
Book Designer:	Lynn Miyata
Typesetter:	Tina Hill
Cover Designer:	Michelle Lee

Contents

To teachers everywhere who have devoted
themselves to improving the lives of our children.
What would we do without you?

Foreword

There is something different about this book: It is useful—really useful. This is not to derogate other books of the genre; there are many good, useful books that can help you over one hurdle or another. However, Vickie Gill is easy to identify with because she speaks plainly and simply of the everyday realities of teaching. If you have been a teacher of difficult-to-reach, difficult-to-teach students, you will find yourself right here in these pages. You will find the real you: the fulfilled, the frustrated, the puzzled, the angry, the grateful. You will find all of your students here, too: the good, the bad, the unbearable, the unforgettable.

Most "help for the teacher" books are grounded in a philosophy—or perhaps more accurately, they espouse one point of view or another concerning behavior and learning. Ms. Gill's work is grounded in an honest love for teaching and children, a sense of calling that reminds us why we teach, and the understanding that even a great teacher needs a plan. Rooted in hard-nosed experience and tempered by logic and kindness, hers is a teaching philosophy that is one part behavior modification, one part child psychology, and one part divine inspiration.

Most teachers cope. They use a variety of tactics borrowed from a variety of authors and professors they had in college. When it comes to dealing with behavior problems, the most commonly taught learning theory is behavior modification. This approach has undergone many evolutions, starting with the highly mechanistic operant conditioning model. Teachers wore wrist counters, and they took data on prebehaviors, the behavior itself, and the consequences of the behavior. Properly implemented, this was a very effective approach. *Properly implemented* is the phrase to focus on. It turns out that it is very difficult to manage such techniques in the hurly-burly of interacting with large groups of students for long periods of time. These techniques have proven so burdensome and difficult, it is now extremely rare to find teachers who can devise individual behavior modification programs, implement them, and take data to demonstrate effectiveness and make revisions. Rather, teachers constantly adapt and modify, searching for the best way to put out their brushfires.

What is a better option? Well, let's revisit behavior modification and see what its latest evolutionary form looks like. It looks like common sense made systematic. It looks like clearly defined roles and expectations for students. It looks like a simple system of classroom management and an empathetic, personal style of teacher-student interaction. It looks exactly like Vickie Gill's classroom. She has been on every side of the education dynamic: rebellious student, overwhelmed new teacher, potential burnout victim, and now master teacher. She speaks with the passionate voice of the true believer.

Full of tactics and techniques, straightforward and interesting, this book is loaded with good examples drawn from Ms. Gill's own trials and errors, but its best contribution may be the expression of a mind-set for successful teachers. It is a mind-set of dedication, empowerment, and positivity that can help fulfill the promise of a teaching career.

Even though I was one of Vickie's professors, I have always learned something when I've visited her classroom. And even though her classmates in graduate school were also master teachers, they all acknowledged they learned from her as well. So will you. Read and enjoy.

James R. Lent
Professor Emeritus,
Vanderbilt University

Preface

I have been teaching high school students how to read, write, and think for almost 20 years. I love my job. If I could afford it, I'd do it for free. So it always distresses me when each year I encounter an increasing number of new teachers who are ready to quit the profession after a couple of months or veteran teachers who are literally enduring until retirement. Their frustration and misery are passed directly on to their students.

I find I spend a great deal of time defending the teaching profession and giving advice to help struggling teachers succeed. One summer, I decided to sit down and organize what I know to be true about good teaching into ten basic attitudes—commandments, if you will. I tried to write as if I were talking to a friend who was having problems in the classroom. Much of what I know I learned through mistakes, but one of the wonders of our profession is that teachers get a chance to review and renew at the beginning of every year.

This book is designed to give new teachers the tools and courage to follow their best instincts about what to do in their own classrooms. It's also dedicated to experienced teachers who are on the edge of burnout to help them remember what made them want to be teachers in the first place.

Since the publication of *The Ten Commandments of Good Teaching*, I've heard from a number of educators who have thanked me for offering practical advice plainly spoken from the voice of experience. For this second edition, I've added an eleventh commandment to illustrate that even the most successful teachers can feel like failures. If you're good at it, teaching is the best job in the world. If you're not good at it, it's a nightmare that affects your mental and physical health. This book is not for those who go into teaching to have their summers free or because they think being a teacher will give them the power they lack in other areas of their lives. This book is for those who fell in love with teaching because they love children and because they truly believe they can positively affect a child's life.

Vickie Gill
Los Olivos, California

About the Author

VICKIE GILL has taught high school English, reading, and journalism for 21 years in both California and Tennessee. She has a B.A. in English from San Jose State University and a M.Ed. from Vanderbilt University. Ms. Gill has won several teaching and community service honors and was a finalist for Tennessee State Teacher of the Year 2000. She is currently teaching English in a small school near Santa Barbara, California. She also conducts workshops for educators on classroom discipline, curriculum development, and the art of teaching. Contact her at *vgill@juno.com* to set up workshops for your school system or to discuss the ideas presented in this book.

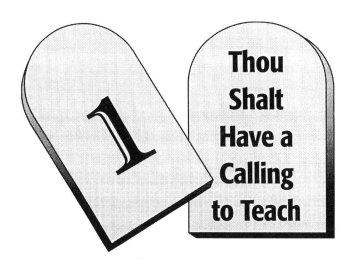

1

Thou Shalt Have a Calling to Teach

Education is what survives when what has been learnt has been forgotten.
—B. F. Skinner

By any means necessary.
—Malcolm X

I became a teacher because I detested school—hated just about every minute of it, particularly from sixth grade on. By the time I was in eighth grade I had a chair of my own right outside the vice-principal's office. I was a teacher's nightmare—the one in the back of the class making noises and comments to make the kids around me laugh. I constantly asked the dreaded question, "Why do we have to learn this junk anyway?" My teachers would warn me not to get smart with them, which always struck me as a contradiction in terms. I would read every book on the suggested reading lists sent home by my English teachers, but I refused to admit that I'd read the books. I didn't want to give them the satisfaction of thinking they had taught me something. I hiked my skirts up, ratted my hair, and sported heavy black eyeliner and white lipstick. When the vice-principal pulled me into her office to wash my face, unroll my skirts, and comb out my hair, I'd march to the closest restroom and redo the whole thing. I was one of the girls who wouldn't let you into the bathrooms at lunch because my friends and I were in there smoking.

In my junior year of high school, my counselor called me in to "discuss my future," one of his minimum job requirements. This man had never taken any notice of me before other than to make big circles around my chair outside the vice-principal's door. He sat me in his office, winced as he perused my rather thick disciplinary file, sighed, and asked me what I planned to do when I grew up. I smiled and told him I was going to be a teacher. He laughed, looked me dead in the eye, and said, "You'll *never* be a teacher." I got up, leaned over his desk, and said, "You don't know me," and walked out of his office.

I understood early on
that I was not
teaching a subject,
I was teaching people.

I'd known I was going to be a teacher since I was five years old—it was the only thing I'd ever wanted to do. Even when I was misbehaving in school, causing a couple of teachers to reconsider their chosen profession, I knew teaching was one of the reasons I was put on this earth. Luckily for me, I had parents who never questioned my goals even when I was at my most rebellious. Because I hated to sit still and listen to lectures, I volunteered to work in Sunday school classes from a very early age, and I knew I had a knack for working with kids. But the main things that helped me to become the teacher I am were all the horrible or ineffectual teachers I observed. I knew there had to be a better way, so I built my teaching career around engaging the students who hated school the most. In my classes, my students are rewarded for asking, "Why do we have to learn this stuff?" This shows they are concerned with their education.

I understood from the beginning I was not teaching a subject, I was teaching people. I believe my attitude toward school would have been very different if I'd had even one teacher who tried to figure out why I was acting like such a jerk. I was obviously intelligent, but they settled for stamping all of my report cards with the phrase "not working up to potential." Not one of them ever asked why. If they had, I would have told them I didn't see the usefulness or the joy in anything they were teaching. It seemed like a complete waste of time to me; one of my teachers even said that high school was a holding zone to keep us teens from glutting the job market. Also, most of my teachers believed students needed to be controlled with a heavy hand, never really understanding the true nature of power.

I did the bare minimum to graduate from high school and paid for my obstinacy by having to attend a junior college for two years. But college was a revelation for me. The teachers didn't care whether I showed up for class because I was paying for the privilege whether or not I showed up. Suddenly, my education became my own. Every class, every credit, was one step closer to my goal, and I blossomed in this atmosphere. Even though it was a painful time for me (and my teachers), my public school experience served me very well in that it taught me what *not* to do as a teacher. For the past 20 years, I've tried to design classes I would like to attend, and it has made all the difference to me and my students.

Sometimes I want to deduct my teaching salary as a charitable contribution on my income tax forms. It's a huge mistake to get into teaching for the money or because summers are free. I've known people who became teachers for these reasons over the years, and they spend the money and the summers trying to recover from the physical and psychological stresses the students cause them. I believe you should become a teacher if you would do it anyway for free. It's one of the hardest jobs I know, requiring you to act as a gifted academician, psychologist, detective, magician, technician, supervisor, entertainer, and counselor all within a class period, and then do it all over again. My favorite thing about teaching is that it stimulates both my creative and practical impulses. I also love that I am solely responsible for the quality of what goes on in my classroom. As you probably have already surmised, I have some serious issues about authority figures. However, as a teacher, I am the authority and no one peers over my shoulder to make sure I'm doing a good job. I am my own quality control, which adds to the pressure and the pleasure of my work.

I consider teachers to be among an elite group of people who can truly change the world.

Teaching is the greatest of all professions. I consider teachers to be among an elite group of people who can truly change the world. I call it the ripple effect. Some time ago, I was talking with a group of people who were in college in the early 1970s, a time of tremendous social upheaval and change. We were laughing about the protest marches, the campus take-overs, and the hubristic attitude that made us believe that if we handed out enough leaflets, the world would slap its collective forehead and shout, "Of course you're right—why didn't I think of peace and love and feeding the children?!" Instead, even after toppling an administration, it was business as usual. One person in the group shook his head at what naive fools we'd been, noting that not one of us had followed an idealistic path. I told him that I had—I'd become a teacher. Instead of trying to change thousands of minds at once, I was influencing people daily in a much smaller arena. It is possible that my students will raise their children with slightly different attitudes about racism, sexism, and their responsibilities to their communities. It's like dropping a pebble in a pool—I can't change everything, but I can help my students to at least examine why they believe what they do and to live a more deliberate life.

You're a closely watched role model who communicates more by what you do than by what you say.

If teaching were easy, anyone could do it. Teachers bear an awesome responsibility because a casual comment by a teacher can become part of a student's life script. How many times have you heard adults say that a teacher's encouragement influenced them to change the course of their lives? On the other hand, I know several adults who speak bitterly of teachers who told them in third grade they were stupid, untalented, or a waste of time; these adults have never forgotten those words. As a teacher, you're not allowed to have such a bad day that you take it out on your students. As a teacher, you're a closely watched role model who communicates more by what you do than by what you say. As a teacher, you are remembered forever, but *how* you are remembered is up to you. Teaching is an incredibly important and demanding job, and it requires a profound commitment. The first commandment of good teaching? Thou shalt not become a teacher unless you feel a calling to this mother of all professions. Depending on your talent and disposition, teaching can be the best or the worst way to earn your living.

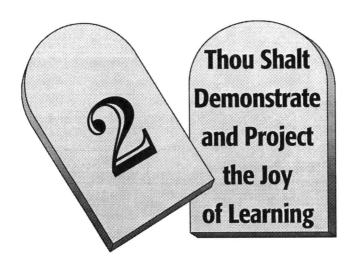

Thou Shalt Demonstrate and Project the Joy of Learning

My husband is a songwriter, so I often attend parties or showcases with people who are not in the field of education. For a long time, I dreaded the moment when someone asked me what I did for a living, because the minute I said I was a teacher, people's attitudes changed toward me. Either their eyes glazed over and they suddenly noticed a long-lost friend across the room, or they straightened up, shifted uncomfortably, and hid their cigarettes behind their backs. If I foolishly added I was an English teacher, all conversation sputtered to a painful end. I realized that the general population's impression is that all teachers are judgmental, anal-retentive control freaks who somehow could deduct points at a cocktail party for poor grammar. Some people I met continued talking to me, complimenting me on sacrificing my life to such a thankless job. It became so annoying, I developed my own defense mechanisms. Sometimes I made a joke and said, "That's right, I ain't gonna tolerate no bad grammar at this here party." Other times, I thanked the person for reducing me to a stereotype and moved on. But the easiest response was to sidestep the question and avoid mentioning teaching at all. What's wrong with this picture? I honestly love my job and am tremendously proud of what I do.

Why do people have the impression that teaching is a boring, joyless profession? Maybe it's because they've all been in boring, joyless classes. I have three daughters who spent 12 years in the public school system. I watched them evolve from ravenous learners to bored participants, fulfilling the minimum requirements to maintain their class rankings. When they were little, they were interested in everything—learning was not compartmentalized, labeled, or evaluated. They did it naturally. When they entered school, they quickly realized that acting average and going along with the program was the easiest way to survive. In most of their classes, they were placed in seats in rows, handed worksheets, and rewarded for not asking why this was happening. My daughters' main goal was to move through the system as quickly as possible so they could get on with "real life." My daughters were very bright young ladies with a great deal of self-control; imagine how painful school is for children with learning disabilities or behavior problems.

Why do people have the impression that teaching is a boring, joyless profession? Maybe it's because they've all been in boring, joyless classes.

But along the way, all my girls had a few remarkable teachers who stood out like beacons in a dense fog. What was different about these people? I believe these teachers clearly demonstrated and projected the joy of learning. Their classes were designed for success, accommodated differences, and gave the impression that magic might break out at any moment. These teachers obviously loved students, viewed them as individuals, and delighted in their uniqueness. These teachers never stopped learning themselves and shared with their students some new discovery or insight that had delighted or amazed them. These teachers made learning so exciting the students didn't want to stay home for fear of missing something really great. These teachers loved what they did, and the students knew it.

I think that one of the hardest things about being a teacher is that we

Take time to remember what drew you to teaching in the first place. What kinds of things did your favorite teachers do?

are constant role models. The students watch everything we do, which can be exhausting. Teaching has a great deal in common with acting and sales. Not only do we need to be completely knowledgeable about the subjects we teach, we also have to make the students want to buy what we're offering. One of the biggest arguments I have ever had with a colleague was whether teachers needed to motivate students. My colleague felt students should come to him predisposed to learn—that was their job. His job was to disseminate the information. I told him the administration would be happy to hear about his attitude. If all this teacher needed to do was disseminate information, we could pass out textbooks, slide a videotape of him at his best into the VCR, and fire his sorry self, thus saving the school system thousands of dollars over the years.

One of the most useful things you can do as a teacher is take time to remember what drew you to teaching in the first place. What kinds of things did your favorite teachers do? What made you fall in love with the subject you teach? What was the atmosphere and layout of your favorite class? Which lessons made an impression on you? What was useful later in your life? Answer these questions, and then monitor yourself as you teach over the years to make sure you include these joyful experiences in your own lessons.

Another tremendous advantage some teachers have is the ability to remember what it's like to be a kid. A few years ago, I attended an in-service workshop with about 50 other teachers from my school district. The presenter asked the teachers to think back to their two most significant memories of high school. He then asked how many of these memories happened inside the classroom. Not one hand was raised. Many of us noted that what really mattered to us in school were sports, social events, broken hearts, cliques, fights, and awards. Most of what we learned academically had long been forgotten unless it was related to the subject we were currently teaching.

A sign in my classroom says, "Education is either to calm the disturbed or disturb the calm."

I have a sign in my classroom that says, "Education is either to calm the disturbed or disturb the calm." This has profoundly affected the way I teach. I discuss this saying with my classes on the first day of school, asking them whether they classify themselves as among the calm or among the disturbed. This usually creates a lively discussion, and I get some immediate insights into some of my students. I point out that many of them have drifted through school for years, sitting quietly, doing whatever was required, questioning nothing, and waiting for the bell to ring. These are the "calm" and my job is to disturb them. I need to make them take charge of their own education, analyzing information rather than just regurgitating it. I work with them in small groups so that they cannot hide in the back of the class; each of them has to defend an answer. I let them know that in my class there is a great tolerance for differences of opinion, but everyone must have an opinion and be able to back it up. Then, I address the "disturbed." These are the students who have what I call "noisy minds." Perhaps their personal lives are in such chaos, they feel the school has nothing to offer of any use. Others are extremely bright students who have become openly hostile to the mediocrity of most classwork. My job is to show them how the skills I'm teaching can help them take control of their lives and futures. My job is to make them think something they have never thought before. My job is to help them turn down the noise in their minds so they can concentrate on the academic skills that will make them successful.

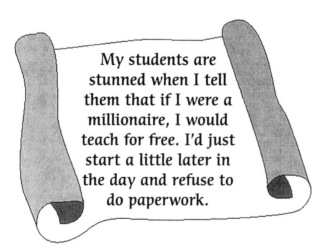

My students are stunned when I tell them that if I were a millionaire, I would teach for free. I'd just start a little later in the day and refuse to do paperwork.

Sometimes I want to thank the few really terrible teachers in the school where I teach because they make my work much easier. These teachers spend so much time boring, humiliating, or trying to control students that when the kids come to my classroom, it's like a breath of fresh air. To many students, my class is a safe, exciting, authentic learning environment where mistakes and handicaps are just useful information. My students are stunned when I tell them that if I were a millionaire, I would teach for free. I'd just start a little later in the day and refuse to do paperwork. Quite often, I'm one of the few adults they know who loves her work. I use this fact as a launching pad for a unit on their goals. I try to help them focus on their calling—on what gives them joy—and determine how to make a living doing it.

Every year I have several students who laugh when I tell them money should not be a deciding factor in choosing a career. They are quite straightforward in pointing out what a sucker I am to settle for teacher's pay. Last year, one senior told me that if it paid enough, he'd be willing to do anything. I suggested that if he were offered one job doing something he loved for $15 an hour and another job doing something he hated for $30 an hour, he'd be a fool to take the higher-paying job. He laughed and said that if the pay was good, he didn't care what he was required to do.

It took only a few minutes to change his mind. I asked him to think about the class in school he had hated the most—the one he thought he'd never pass because it was so boring and the teacher was so awful. Then I told him I'd pay him $30 an hour to sit in that class all day every day for the next 30 years. That got his attention. How could a person who became a teacher because of the love of a subject or a desire to help young people design a class so abhorrent that this student would cut his salary in half for the rest of his life to avoid it?

Human beings are born to learn. Babies do it so naturally, it's almost impossible to keep them from it. Ask kindergartners about their future plans and they shout out an eclectic set of goals involving careers as singers-doctors-astronauts-veterinarians-preachers-mommies-on-the-side. Ask a group of high school students what they want to do for a living and it's likely the majority of them shrug their shoulders and mutter, "I don't know." What happened in those 12 years? The second commandment of good teaching? Thou shalt demonstrate and project the joy of learning.

Thou Shalt Keep Your Eyes on the Prize

Now that I've tried to inspire you with the best that teachers can be, just how do you create such a class? How do you choose what to teach? In a course I took in graduate school, the instructor asked, "What's worth knowing?" The class was full of teachers working on master's degrees, and I could tell many of them felt this was a stupid question. But I found it exhilarating. It really caused me to examine what I was teaching. Earlier I mentioned getting into trouble in a class for asking why we had to learn what the teacher was presenting. To me, that should be the most significant question the teacher addresses. If you plan to design your class around your state's prepared curriculum, then be sure you have an answer to that question. The following answers are not okay:

▶ Your teacher next year will expect you to know this.
▶ Because I told you so.
▶ You'll be asked this material on a test.
▶ This is what every class at this level is studying.
▶ It's none of your business.
▶ I had to suffer through this, so should you.

Recently, I asked four honor students who excelled in advanced math how they might use what they'd learned. The best answer was they may

13

need it later in life. Not one of them could tell me how they could use the math they had learned even though they were glad they'd taken the classes. I think the reason so little of what students study in school stays with them is because no one has demonstrated the usefulness of the information. My husband uses geometry and algebra to design decks, but he admits when he was learning those skills in high school, he had no idea they could be applied to construction. In my experience, I never really learned anything until I had to use it. Good teachers provide practical applications for the facts they're presenting so they prepare their students to be more than great Trivial Pursuit players.

> I never really learned anything until I had to use it. Good teachers provide practical applications for the facts they're presenting.

Whenever I design a curriculum, I always ask myself what I want the students to be able to do when they leave the class. In other words, I start from the big picture and then work backward. If I want them to be able to write a college-level research paper, I break that objective down into all the skills they need to accomplish it. If I want them to know how to communicate effectively on a job, I think about everything promoting that skill.

I also ask my students on the first day of class, "What are the characteristics of an educated person?" We toss around ideas for a while, and I write all their responses on the board. Usually, they include items such as having a big vocabulary or reading Shakespeare as signs of an educated person. I always ask if the ability to fix a car engine or design a house might label a person as "educated." After much dissension, I try to lead them to consider the following attributes:

▶ Educated people can find out what they need to know.

▶ Educated people share a common body of knowledge with other educated people that aids them in finding out what they need to know.

▶ Educated people are curious; they are lifelong learners.

In simplified forms, these are my three main teaching goals. Of course, in reality these goals are huge, especially when students enter my class completely uninterested in finding out anything, with an uncommonly small body of knowledge, and with a real distaste for learning. But it's a starting place.

What are the characteristics of an educated person?

Another sign in my room says, "If you find what is within you, what you find will save you; if you do not find what is within you, what you do not find will destroy you." Many of the lessons I teach are designed to help students discover what they are meant to do. I know this sounds beyond the realm of what schools should be required to do, but until students focus on some personal goals, most of what they learn in your class will be forgotten after the final exam.

The only adults
in the world who
are ever asked to
identify nouns
and verbs are
English teachers.

I'm blessed because I teach English—the greatest of all subjects because it involves reading, writing, and thinking. These three skills are so flexible, I can create a curriculum to address almost any need my students may have. For example, I begin every semester with a unit on personal goals. This unit enables me to pretest my students' writing skills by having them write about their plans for the next 10 years. The result is a fairly accurate picture of the students' writing abilities and the kind of work they need to reach their goals. It also sets up a discussion topic of high interest for the first small-group meetings. The students who are already focused can share their plans, and the clueless ones can start considering some options. During this unit, the students complete a computer program that suggests possible careers based on their responses to questions about their interests, skills, and plans. This software program also gives up-to-date information about job requirements, salaries, training, and availability. It includes a database of colleges throughout the state and information about getting into those colleges. We do all sorts of personality and interest analysis sheets, constantly trying to match each student to a career. The students eventually write letters to colleges researching financial aid and admission requirements. We have speakers from various businesses telling students about their jobs and, more important, about what they expect from employees. Please note no "busywork" is assigned during this unit. The usefulness of everything they do is obvious to the students as they discover the power of the written word through writing letters and learn to tackle the puzzle of their futures.

I know most of the curriculum frameworks you receive from state departments of education start with big goals that are then broken down into objectives. But quite often, teachers focus so much on moving through the objectives, they lose sight of the big picture. When I began teaching in Tennessee, the English Department chairperson of my school and I heatedly disagreed over what should be taught in a high school English class. She insisted I should work from the state-adopted grammar and literature textbooks, moving through the objectives in exactly the same time frame as other English teachers. I pointed out that it was not unusual for me to have students in my senior English class who had done precious little writing because of this inflexible focus on the parts rather than the whole. She countered that the students had to master basic grammatical skills before they could possibly hope to write a composition. I asked my chairperson how she thought a baby should be taught to walk. Should we put the child in a high chair and show him or her diagrams of the leg, requiring him to memorize the names of all of the moving parts? Should we show films of people walking to the baby? Or should we put the baby on the floor and let him or her stumble and fall again and again until one day the baby stays up? This is exactly what we do when we teach writing.

In terms of the big picture, the only adults in the world who are ever asked to identify nouns and verbs are English teachers. Everyone else just unconsciously uses these parts of speech. Students need to write and write and write some more. They need to write letters that are really mailed and compositions that analyze their opinions. They need to read articles about marriage and parenting and write responses describing what they will do in these relationships. These topics and projects are not only of high interest to students, they are essential to the students' futures. I further annoyed my chairperson during our conversation by pointing out that if I ever needed to take a year off from teaching for whatever reason, I'd just pass out the grammar books, give a 15-minute lecture on nouns and verbs, and then have the students do problems 1 to 50 at the end of the chapter while I kick back at my desk. There is so little time and so much to do in a class period, we must focus on the most effective methods available. If a student has been using grammar and spelling texts for 10 years and still doesn't get it, then this is an ineffectual use of time and we should try something else.

Choosing goals on the first day of a semester forces the students to take responsibility for what will go on in my class.

I need to tell you at this point that I do teach to tests. In my reading/writing labs, I have students who will not graduate from high school unless they pass the state competency test. But I make this their choice. On the first day of the semester, I pass out a sheet with a long list of goals—things I can teach relating to reading, writing, and thinking. One of the goals is to pass the competency test. I then ask the students to place a checkmark next to all the things they'd like to tackle during the semester. Finally, I ask them to circle the three goals of most importance to them.

I believe this activity accomplishes two things. One, it tells me what my students think they need to know. I can then group students with common goals. Two, it forces the students to take responsibility for what happens in my class. It gives them a sense of ownership and that they are not simply empty vessels into which I will pour what I think they need.

You would be amazed at how this activity increases the students' focus—and their discomfort. Some of the students don't want to admit they are in school to learn anything at all. They see school as a holding zone, keeping them from enjoying "real life." Last year, I passed out the goal sheets to a group of 9th-, 10th-, and 11th-grade students in my reading lab. When I collected the sheets, one boy handed me a blank sheet of paper, with nothing but his name on top. He looked at me defiantly, hoping for his first skirmish to establish the battle lines. Instead, I glanced at the paper, gazed at him fondly, and murmured, "This is wonderful." He shifted uncomfortably and said, "What do you mean?" I smiled and answered that by not checking anything, he was telling me he wanted to learn everything and he was my favorite kind of student. I told him I appreciated his confidence in me and that I'd do everything I could to help him succeed. He eyed me suspiciously for a while, but he was mine for the rest of the class.

This is why the first week of school is so hectic. I have to find out what my students need before I can create the objectives.

Preparing for state competency tests is extremely boring for both teachers and students. However, when it's the students' choice, it adds new energy and dedication to the pursuit of this goal. Because the test takes place about six weeks after the semester begins, I make this an intensive, all-out attack, with the promise of much more interesting reading, writing, and thinking activities after the test is over. Imagine—reading, writing, and thinking are the rewards the students look forward to.

A few years ago, one of my supervisors asked to see the objectives for my reading lab for the following year. He called me at home in July and said he needed to see what I would be teaching for a state department form he was completing. I told him I could not possibly know my objectives until I met my students. This just stunned him, and he accused me of teaching without a plan. I told him I could easily hand him a beautifully sequenced set of objectives lifted straight from the state's curriculum guide for the basic competency test—this would be no problem. But what if, when I met my students in the fall, 90% of them had passed the competency test? What if some couldn't read at all? What if some were fairly good writers, but they hated reading? What if some had such severe emotional problems, they couldn't even sit still? I explained to my supervisor this is why the first week of school is so hectic—I have to find out what my students need before I can create the objectives. However, I did add that my main goal was to turn out educated persons, told him the three characteristics of an educated person, and suggested he write that on his form.

When deciding what to teach, you have to trust your instincts. I can picture several of my former supervisors shifting uneasily in their chairs thinking of those incompetent teachers who show movies all day or let the students sit and talk as long as they leave the teacher alone. My response is that these people are not teachers and should not be in the profession. If someone so incompetent has been hired and has maintained his or her job through tenure, then it's the principal's problem to ensure that at least the state's guidelines are followed. But it is not the principal's job to tamper with authentic teaching that works. Figure out what you want your students to be able to do when they leave your class, make sure these objectives match what they need to be successful in life, and pass on the joy of learning that made you choose your subject in the first place. You need to be original and teach in the style that works best for you. The third commandment of good teaching? Thou shalt know where you are going and keep your eyes on the prize.

Thou Shalt Be Organized and Accountable

I'm a big believer in the old saying that luck happens when preparation meets opportunity. Most people who are really good at what they do work really hard, and what I'm about to suggest in this chapter will definitely present a challenge to you. Now that you've captured the vision of what you want to teach—the big picture—the next task is to brainstorm all of the steps that take the students to those goals. After that, you need to identify the best ideas, sequence them into teaching units, and then plan activities that demonstrate and promote the skills the students will need to reach the original goals.

When brainstorming, allow yourself to be completely nonjudgmental—no idea is too silly or too difficult. Leave yourself open to everything. Some of my best teaching ideas come from the oddest places. I constantly rip quotes, addresses, or articles out of magazines and newspapers. I subscribe to English and adolescent literary journals. I tape almost everything I watch on TV so I can stop the program and write down a quote or an idea. I participate in an Internet discussion group about the teaching of reading and writing. I constantly ask people I meet from all walks of life to identify the most useful things they learned in school. I interview employers and personnel directors to find out what they want us to teach in the schools. And I read all sorts of things to keep up on what is going on in the world.

One of the major goals I have for my senior English students is for them to write a college-level research paper using the word processors in my classroom. To prepare the students for this project, I introduce them to the techniques of research through a unit on debate. Their first assignment is to outline and write a four-paragraph paper presenting both sides of a controversial issue. Through this assignment, I can show them how to write an introduction, conclusion, and supporting points, and how to separate themselves from a topic. I quote F. Scott Fitzgerald, who said that "a great mind can hold two conflicting thoughts at the same time." I tell the students that they can never really win a debate until they thoroughly understand the beliefs of the opposition. I point out this skill will serve them well in their relationships at home and on the job. This is an amazingly difficult assignment for some students but an enlightening experience. After they research the topic and we review their rough drafts, they use the word processors to create a composition without errors.

Meanwhile, I prepare them for an actual debate. The class votes on two or three controversial issues, and I let them select the topic of their choice. The only catch is that they don't know which side of the issue they will be defending until the day before the debate. At this point, the assignment really gets interesting and some real learning occurs. Often, students are highly opinionated about a number of topics, but they haven't a clue as to what the opposition will say. Sometimes during this activity, I can literally see their minds open.

A number of years ago, one of my students in senior English was the most overtly racist person I had ever met. His racism ran so deep that when he said highly offensive things in class, he didn't have that look of defiance sported by most people trying to shock others. He really believed that the grass was green, the sun was hot, and nonwhites were inferior. He and I had already exchanged some heated sentiments about this during the semester, and when it came time to choose debate topics, he raised his hand, smirked at his buddies, and suggested that all blacks should be sent back to Africa. I never missed a beat and wrote his topic on the board with the others.

He generated enough support in the class to have his topic voted as one of the three to be debated the following week. He kept waiting for me to argue with him or censor his suggestion, but I just set up the debates as usual. On the day before the debate, the eight students who signed up for his topic gathered before me to draw "for" and "against" slips from a basket on my desk. As luck would have it, he drew an "against" paper. He was furious, but I told him that I had honored his input, and now it was his turn to honor the rules of the debate. Most of his friends predicted that he would not show up the next day, but he was there, he was prepared, and he dazzled the audience. He argued passionately and intelligently for racial harmony and equality, and we were stunned. His team won the debate and he made sure everyone knew he was just doing it for the grade. But for a moment, I knew he at least had examined both sides of an opinion he'd never questioned since he was a child. I have no idea if he ever softened his views or changed his actions in any way, but I was extremely proud of him for those 15 minutes, and I believe he never forgot the experience.

I believe that for every objective you choose to teach, you can design meaningful, exciting, and authentic activities to reach your goal.

This debate unit takes about two weeks of the semester, but as you can see, a myriad of valuable skills are practiced in a dynamic atmosphere designed to engage every student. Most of the employers I talk with want us to teach basic reading, writing, math, computer, communication, and teamwork skills. This unit covers everything but the math. I believe that for every objective you choose to teach, you can design meaningful, exciting, and authentic activities to reach your goal. In my reading lab, I work with many students who are reading anywhere from 2 to 10 years below their grade level. Some of these students are parents, and a few are even married.

Because most have some sort of learning disability, it is very likely they will pass this struggle with the printed word on to their children. So, in the course of teaching them to read, I also teach them how to teach someone else to read. For example, I have some students who need to review basic phonetic principles, such as short vowel sounds, and this can be humiliating for a 16-year-old. When I begin the class, I tell my students that at the end of the semester, we will be going to a primary school three times a week to tutor little kindergarten through second-grade students. Therefore, they need to pay close attention to everything I show them, because they will be assigned a student of their own to teach. This really gets their attention. As I work with the group studying vowel sounds, I also demonstrate to them how to teach their own children to read. After years of working with this cross-age tutoring program, I'm not convinced my students dramatically raise the reading levels of the primary school children. But I do know these experiences have raised my students' reading levels and have provided a healthy boost to their self-esteem.

This brings us to one of the most important characteristics of good teaching: You must develop a system to document what you do. Every year, I work with students who have received passing grades in all their English classes as well as the state competency test. The only problem is that they can barely read and write. I don't believe a list of grades is a useful indicator of a student's progress. As a supplement, I keep a portfolio for each of my students. I know this sounds like just more paperwork, but it's the most accurate way I can demonstrate what a student has accomplished in my class. For example, the portfolios of my senior English students contain a set of pretests (writing, reading, comprehension, spelling, listening, goals, etc.) and several assignments done in class on the word processors that are relatively error-free, including a cover letter and résumé, as well as several typed essays. At the end of the semester, I give each student a large envelope containing examples of their early work and their perfect papers, including three copies of their résumés and their corrected research paper. I tell them to put this envelope in their underwear drawers for safekeeping, because every paper will be useful to them later in college or when they look for a job. This is amazing to most of them. They often comment that this was the first class in which they could clearly see what they had accomplished and the first class in 12 years that required them to do something again and again until it was perfect.

So how do you keep up with the constant correcting and monitoring that this system requires? My solution is to work with my students in three small groups. The maximum number of students in my reading lab is 15 per class, and I've convinced my administrators to put no more than 25 students in my English classes. My school has adopted the four-period-day schedule, requiring me to teach three classes a day. Each class period is 90 minutes, so I meet with each small group for about 25 minutes per class period. As I'm meeting with one group, the second group is working on the computers, using writing, spelling, vocabulary, or career software. The students in the third group are in their seats (at tables in my class) working on the assignment they will be bringing to me to discuss or correct in a few minutes.

I often think that for many of my students, I'm one of the few adults with whom they have a meaningful conversation all day.

This system accomplishes a number of things. First, it creates a businesslike atmosphere in the class—everyone is working all the time and a cardinal rule is the class must be quiet enough so the group working with me is not disturbed. I often tell the students if I'm working, you're working, and I teach all period. Second, the small groups create informal settings in which students can take risks and get individual attention from me. Third, I can assign a great deal of writing because I can quickly rotate each student to the chair on my right to review the assignment immediately. We jokingly call my pen the "laser pen," capable of finding errors in anything. But the atmosphere is light and respectful, and I can go over errors with the students rather than handing back compositions covered with red ink that proves only that the teacher is very good at proofreading. This is when I offer the students minilessons on grammar and structure. Fourth, this is a great way for me to get to know my students as individuals. A student can't remain invisible in my class; I counted on that sense of invisibility in classes when I was a teenager and causing so many disruptions. I often think that for many of my students, I'm one of the few adults with whom they have a meaningful conversation all day. Finally, my system largely eliminates many techniques most students have mastered by high school: copying someone else's homework and uncanny peripheral vision. I rarely assign worksheets or questions from the textbook, so I can tell very quickly when someone is trying to pass off another student's work as his or her own.

A few years ago, I worked with a difficult young man who had become very good at passing classes by forcing other students to share homework or test answers. It took some time for me to convince him that (a) I read every piece my students write, sometimes several times, and (b) I'm not an idiot. I knew he'd been goofing off on the computers, but when his group came to the board, he turned in a beautiful, one-page, double-spaced composition about his career goals. He'd accessed another student's word processing file, deleted her name, and added his own. Evidently, several of his previous teachers had graded papers by weighing or measuring something, and he'd been rewarded with passing grades. As I glanced over the paper, I immediately remembered where I had seen it before, so I found the girl's portfolio and pulled both the students into the hallway. I gave the girl a wink as I pretended to lambaste her for turning in plagiarized work. I purposely didn't look directly at the boy, but I could see his face getting redder and redder as the girl protested her innocence. Finally, he admitted copying her paper, and I advised him to read enough next time to at least know that his topic sentence proudly announced his plans to become a cosmetologist. He became a pretty good worker after that.

To use this small-group system of managing classes, you have to be extremely organized. My daily lesson plans are written in pencil in case they need to be revised. I've designed a chart showing me at a glance what each group should be doing during the 25-minute sessions. The seat assignments are written on a chalkboard at the back of the class, and the necessary materials are laid out before the day begins. I usually plan in two-week cycles, testing vocabulary or spelling skills on the 14th day. At this time, the students staple all their work together in a very specific order, using a list assignment I distribute. Most work has been corrected in the small-group meetings, so I quickly average the grades and put one grade in my roll book. On that day, we often have a large-group meeting during which we discuss what we've learned over the past two weeks and plans for the next two weeks. Other than the first week of school, these periodic large-group meetings are the only times I work with the class as a whole. In addition, twice each month, I give the students free time during the last 30 to 45 minutes of the period to play the normally forbidden computer games or work on a project of their choice while I correct the tests and record the grades. I used to feel guilty about this unstructured time, but I built it into the system so I didn't have to stay after school or work on weekends just to keep up with grading. It is also one of the few times I can talk casually with students about personal problems or what's going on in their lives.

There is always something for the students to do, and they get very individualized attention.

Because I work with the students for only 25 minutes per group, it's very important that I have the full time with them. This system eliminates many behavior problems because there is always something for the students to do and they get very individualized attention, which increases their chances for success. To give my group my undivided attention, I assign "contact persons" for each group. I do this at the end of the first week of class because by then it's fairly obvious which students know something about the computers, have reasonable social skills, and can follow instructions. Students who have trouble on the computers or with the seatwork know to quietly ask their contact person before asking me. A vast majority of the problems can be handled this way, allowing me to work with my small group undisturbed.

Besides the test and classwork grades, I also put a double participation grade in the roll book every two weeks. This is determined by a daily chart I keep indicating how students worked during the class period. Each day when the students leave, I quickly mark a plus, a check, or a minus next to their names. A plus means they worked all period and were prepared when they came to the small group to work with me. A check means I had to speak to them to remind them to get to work or they caused a slight disturbance in the class, but got right back to work. A minus means they had a bad day, getting little done, sleeping, or causing such a disturbance I had to divert my attention from the small group to deal with their problems. These marks break down into numerical values: A plus equals 10 points; a check means 5 points; and a minus signifies 0 points, with a possible perfect score of 100. I give the grade a double value because it rewards the students in the class who have poor English skills and really struggle with their classwork and tests but work hard every day to improve. It also challenges students who come to the class with excellent English skills but are used to doing only what is necessary to get by. These latter students can ace a test but waste a tremendous amount of time, usually disturbing other people while they do it. Also, these students will make the worst kinds of employees unless they learn that they will be paid based on their efforts and that their job is to stay busy. Sometimes the kids beg for a free day or a movie or something. I tell them they've already mastered movie viewing, sitting around talking, and sleeping. In fact, most of them could earn a Ph.D. in those areas. I point out it would be an insult to them for me to teach objectives they've already mastered. Let's get to work.

Teaching can eat up your life—it is very possible to spend all day and night in your school trying to help everyone and keeping up with your work.

Getting organized pays off for you in a number of ways. Your students then have confidence in what you're teaching because you have an agenda and know specifically where you're going. There is always something meaningful to do if you have to substitute one activity for another. You eliminate a huge proportion of discipline problems because you don't spend the first part of each class scrambling to find materials that you forgot to prepare. Also, if parents or administrators have questions about a student's grades or work, you have the documentation at your fingertips. Finally, you put in less overtime because you've developed a system that works within the given time constraints. Remember that teaching can eat up your life—it is very possible to spend all day and night in your school trying to help everyone and keeping up with your work. You can never give enough. As passionate as I am about my job, I have a life away from the classroom that is equally important and needs to be protected. This life not only shields me from burnout, it also makes me a more interesting, well-rounded role model for my students. The fourth commandment of good teaching? Thou shalt be organized and accountable for your students' success.

Thou Shalt Ask and Ye May Receive

Up to this point, I've tried to describe teaching as a visionary's job that can wear you out. You may be ready to shout "Check, please!" and look for employment in the recreation and leisure field. But there are ways to make your life as a teacher much easier. The most useful method is to figure out specifically the tools you need to do the best job you can and then ask for them. The worst thing that can happen is someone says no and you have to seek elsewhere or modify your plans. But it's been my experience that people say yes more often than no, and that those who get are those who ask.

Quite often a colleague will come into my classroom to borrow something or to ask my advice. This is usually a teacher who is struggling with his or her students. During the course of our conversation, this person often says, "Well, I could be doing a good job, too, if I had this big room and all of these computers." Sometimes the comment is designed to make me feel guilty for my wealth, but it doesn't work. I have 10 computers, five printers, a scanner, and a phone line in my room because I asked for them. They didn't. I'm not so naive as to think that all my colleagues need to do is run to the front office and hand the principal a list of items they want for their classrooms. This probably won't work, although I've gotten a number of things I've needed by describing to my principal the really cool project I'm working on that would bring glory and honor to his school, if I only had a certain piece of equipment or if he'd pay to send me to a conference somewhere. I've been taken aback a number of times by how easily the principal has agreed. I admit that it is a good idea to keep an ear to the ground about what's going on elsewhere in the school, and the bookkeeper or secretaries can be incredibly helpful in choosing the right moment to approach the administrator. It also helps if you have proved to be an effective and useful teacher. But the point is that you never get what you need unless you ask. "No" is not a rejection, just a detour.

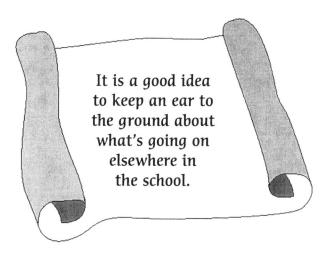

It is a good idea to keep an ear to the ground about what's going on elsewhere in the school.

When I was designing my class, I knew I needed to have enough computers so I could work with the students in groups. I already had a few computers that my brother, who works for IBM, had helped me acquire, but they were discontinued models and woefully out of date. One day, I was in a teachers' meeting and the principal was describing a new system the counselors would be using to help students plan for their futures. All eighth graders would be required to choose either a "college prep" or a "tech prep" track when choosing classes to take in high school. The goal was to raise the requirements for graduation and eliminate the situation where a student is handed a diploma but is prepared for neither college nor work. The state department of education had mandated that the schools raise the requirements and quality of all high school classes to avoid the embarrassment of graduates who couldn't read their diplomas.

This great idea gave me a great idea. I wrote a proposal for a Reading/ Writing Lab designed to help students increase their skills to the point where they could succeed in these more challenging classes. When I presented my proposal to the school board, I emphasized that it would be imprudent to require more from the students without offering support classes to get them up to par. Therefore, I was offering my services as the coordinator of this new reading lab to help ensure a quality education for all graduates. All I needed to accomplish this were some up-to-date computers. The board promised to get back to me, and I held my breath. A few weeks later, the technology coordinator called to say the board had approved my plan, and the superintendent wanted to know how many computers I needed. I'd been around the block with this sort of thing before, so I asked for twice as many as I wanted. "Ten," I said. She said, "OK, anything else?" I almost fainted, but recovered quickly. "And five printers!" "OK, anything else?" Now I was scrambling. "And software and paper!" She told me she'd get the order right out and the equipment would be delivered to my classroom by the beginning of the school year. I was stunned. They were giving me far more than I expected just because I asked.

I was stunned.
They were giving
me far more
than I expected
just because
I asked.

Later, when I was assigned to teach a journalism class, I was able to get a phone in my room. Few teachers in my school have phones in their rooms, and this has always been a real inconvenience. However, it is usually considered too much an expense to be justified. I told my principal my journalism students needed to sell ads and interview people in the community as part of their classwork, and a phone was essential for a class such as this. I also pointed out the yearbook office had a phone. This kind of association can be very useful, which is why it's important to stay aware of what is going on in the school. It was certainly the deciding factor for me, and a phone line was installed the following week. It's important to note that I wouldn't have become angry if my principal had said no, and I certainly wouldn't have given up. Asking the principal was just the first step.

Years ago, I read a book called *Games People Play* by Eric Berne (1964). I found the ideas in this book very useful in dealing with students, teachers, parents, and administrators, even though it was not written specifically for educators. One of the games it describes is "Wooden Leg." People who play this game always have excuses for their inability to do something they want or need to do. For example, they may say, "I could really teach history if it weren't for these awful kids," or "I could try some more interesting things in my classes if it weren't for the administrators," or "There'd be no stopping me if I could only get the money from the school board," and on and on. It is true that sometimes great ideas are stifled because of lack of funds or support, but I don't believe in making excuses. Either do it or don't, but for heaven's sake, don't whine about it. That not only doesn't help the situation, but it makes you look impotent to the other staff members.

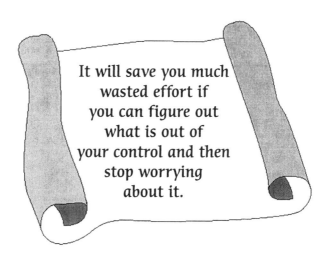

It will save you much wasted effort if you can figure out what is out of your control and then stop worrying about it.

I have a large poster of the famous prayer that reminds us that true wisdom is knowing the difference between the things we can do something about and the things we can't do anything about. I teach a whole lesson based on this philosophy. I tell my students they are not victims, and they can choose whether or not to live with a problem. When you're working in a school, it saves you much wasted effort if you can figure out what is out of your control and then stop worrying about it. In the same manner, figure out what is within your control and take some action.

Another game described in *Games People Play* is called "Yes, but." It goes like this. Someone comes to you with a problem, and you offer several possible solutions. However, after each suggestion, the other person says, "Yes, but . . ." and tells you why he or she can't do what you've suggested. I will play this game through three "yes, but," and then I realize that the person does not want to solve the problem; he or she wants to complain about it. After such an experience, I just listen or move on.

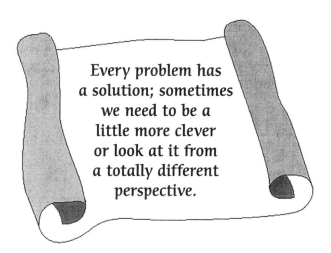

Every problem has a solution; sometimes we need to be a little more clever or look at it from a totally different perspective.

I have a friend who is a firm believer in visualization—physically and mentally creating a very specific image of what it is you want. She believes that when you become this focused, what you need will come to you. It's happened many times in her life. This doesn't mean that you just sit around and wish. Quite often I've stumbled on solutions to problems by mentioning what I need to a wide variety of people. The people who work in schools can be amazingly resourceful, and you'll be surprised at the connections they have outside the system. Some of the most valuable resources available to you are the janitors, maintenance personnel, and secretaries in your school. They know far more than you ever will about what is going on in the school, and they can make your life a lot easier.

Students and parents will also amaze you. Last year, I wanted to build another light table for my journalism class but couldn't find a piece of glass thick enough. I mentioned this to my senior English students and one boy shouted, "My daddy works for Ford Motors—we'll get you that glass!" I've had students bring in printer paper and other office supplies donated by their parents (I always double-check with their folks to make sure it really is "donated."). I've asked parents to speak to classes about their professions, and sometimes they connect me with someone who works in a field my students are researching. I've also had many useful items donated by community businesses that are glad to support local schools. I practice what I preach to my students and write letters to anyone who can possibly help me do the best job I can. When a letter is answered, I share it with my students to point out the power of the written word. The worst thing that can happen is that the request is denied.

If you're a new teacher, listen to students, teachers, and other personnel talk about other teachers in the school. Fairly soon you'll hear someone's name come up over and over because of interesting things going on in his or her class or because that person is involved in the decision-making processes of the school. Go to this teacher and ask for help. I guarantee that 99% of the time, the teacher is delighted to share information, materials, and advice. Some schools have a mentoring system in place already, but if your school doesn't, find your own mentor. I've had teachers sit in on my classes during their planning periods to observe the system I've created or to learn how to work with students with learning or behavior problems. This has never bothered me, and I'm honored they asked. I really believe in being kind and helpful to everyone I can because I know I'll need help myself in the future. I've cleared some of my biggest hurdles by calling in favors from people I'd helped in the past. The Internet is another resource that has become available in the past few years. It's fairly simple to connect with people working in the same field as you who may have very practical answers to your questions. Every problem has a solution; sometimes we need to be a little more clever or look at it from a totally different perspective. What's the fifth commandment of good teaching? Ask and ye just may receive.

Thou Shalt Be Fair and Prepared

Now that you have your vision, your lesson plans, and the equipment you need, how in the heck do you get the little hoodlums to sit down and listen to you? I'll be honest—I think discipline is the biggest challenge you face in the classroom, and it is surely the Achilles' heel of most new teachers. I've been teaching for many, many years, and you can tell that I love my job. However, when I started out, I wanted to quit because I was sure I'd never get the students to behave. It was without a doubt my weakest point. Now I consider it one of my strengths. What happened?

In the beginning, I did not understand the nature of power or control. I had heard all the advice passed down for generations about not smiling until Christmas, starting out tough but easing up as the class progresses, and treating the kids as they treat you. These gems may work for some people, but they were useless for me. I had two problems with this advice from the beginning: (a) I wanted the students to enjoy my class, and (b) I remember what I did as a kid to teachers who were inflexible control freaks.

In my experience, mere force just doesn't work. My problem was that the kids would behave fairly well for a while, but they would push for more and more freedom, and the class would end in chaos with both the students and me glad to see the other leave. I often left school in tears and dreaded going back the next day. After a great deal of experience, I realized I was doing two things wrong. First, the students could tell I was apologetic that we had rules and unsure about what I was doing. Second, I made threats I didn't back up. The students saw right through me and, human nature being what it is, they wrestled for control of the class. What was interesting was that none of us was very happy about that. This was my first clue: Children like to know there is someone in charge—someone who has their best interests at heart and who has a plan. I grew up hating rules, but I came to realize there are very few human interactions that can function without them.

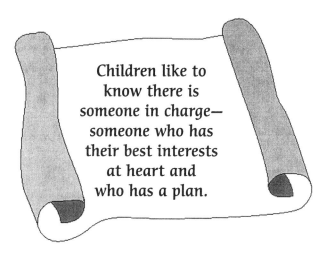

Children like to know there is someone in charge—someone who has their best interests at heart and who has a plan.

Some time ago, one of my reading classes was not going well. Partly because of the mix of students in the class, many of whom had learning and behavioral disabilities, I felt I was spending more time than usual just keeping the kids in line. Instead of placing blame or coming down on the students with an iron fist, I found a solution where I least expected it. I was reading the monthly magazine of the National Education Association, which focuses on what teachers are doing across America. In it was a short profile of a history teacher with a unique way of getting his students to understand the need for laws in this country. A light went on in my head, and I planned a similar activity for the next day. As the reading students filed into the room, I waited until they were all seated and told them that I'd been unhappy with the way the class was going. This caused a sigh, and they all took the slumping posture of students who know they are about to be chewed out by an authority figure. I said I considered it my fault (faces shot up all over the room) and I realized I had been too rule oriented and needed to lighten things up (suspicion rippled in their eyes). I suggested that instead of getting right into our regular work, we should play a game. I had everyone stand up and form a large circle around the room. Meanwhile, I pulled a beach ball out from behind my desk. Without giving any directions, I threw the ball at a student. He looked at me, puzzled, but I just smiled and said, "Go ahead!" He shrugged his shoulders and threw the ball at another student. Ignoring the comments about my sanity, I arbitrarily pointed at a student and commanded him or her to sit down. I continued to do this after every few tosses of the ball, and soon only one boy was left standing. I congratulated him on being the winner and asked him if he wanted to play again. He told me that this was the most ignorant game he'd ever played. I looked hurt and asked him why—I'd had fun. He pointed out that no one knew what to do; they were all just throwing a stupid ball. Another chimed in that there was no winner because they didn't know what I expected. I looked confused and asked what they meant. Bless his heart, one of the most rebellious students in the class shouted out, "We couldn't play right because there were no rules." The last word kind of died on his lips because even though he was one of the most famous behavior problems in the school, he was also very smart. I grinned and innocently asked, "So, you're saying that for a group of people to really have fun, there need to be some guidelines?" The point was quickly taken, and we had a good talk about the rules of my class and the logic behind them. As students moved to join their groups, I heard one of them say, "I told you she was tricky."

Your class needs rules, but they have to be *your* rules, based on what creates order in your room and enhances the learning experience. In my school, every teacher is required to submit an assertive discipline plan to the vice-principal at the beginning of the semester. New teachers are given a sample copy to use, and it amazes me how many of them just copy down the generic rules and consequences and turn those in. Granted, there are some tried-and-true rules that work well, such as "come prepared to work." That covers a lot of territory, from bringing supplies to paying attention. But only an inexperienced teacher would put "No talking" on a rule sheet. That rule is a setup for failure.

How do I know? Well, let's go back to my best training ground for teaching—my old high school. I once had a teacher who taught English and home economics, and unfortunately for her, I was in both classes. This woman gave the impression of being nervous and angry, and she definitely did not understand the nature of control. I figured I had sized her up within the first 10 minutes of class, and she seemed like fair game. She had yelled at several students already, including me, and I knew she'd be an easy mark.

Your class needs rules, but they have to be your rules, based on what creates order in <u>your</u> room and enhances the learning experience.

As expected, she sat us in rows and she stood at the front. I used my usual strategy of sitting in the back of the class and hiding behind someone with big hair. This gave me a lot of leeway. She had the rules of her class posted on the front chalkboard, and the minute I saw "No talking" and "Do not get up out of your seat," I knew I was home free. The first time she turned her back to write something on the board, I tossed my pen about three feet from my desk, then waved my hand frantically in the air. When she turned around, she eyed me with disgust and asked what I wanted. I smiled and innocently asked her to please come pick up my pen for me because I was just trying to follow her rules and I couldn't ask the person next to me because we couldn't talk and I couldn't get it myself because we couldn't get out of our seats and would she please get it for me now? The class froze as her eyes narrowed and blood started rushing to her cheeks, but she knew I had her. Glaring at me, she marched to the back of the room, picked up my pen, and slammed it on my desk. I smiled my most angelic smile and thanked her profusely. As she made her way back to the front, I tossed the pen three feet in the other direction. When she turned around to continue her lecture, there I was, waving my hand again. By now her voice was cracking when she asked what I wanted this time. I acted all flustered and said I didn't know what was wrong with me, maybe I was just so excited to be back in school or something, but I dropped my pen again and would she please come get it for me because I couldn't talk and I couldn't get out of my seat. That did it. She screamed, "Come with me, young lady!" and marched me down to the principal's office. She told the principal that I was acting up in class, and he asked me to tell him what I'd done. I looked puzzled and said, "I don't know, I was just trying to follow her rules. She told us we couldn't talk or get out of our seats and I dropped my pen and asked her to get it for me." He turned to the teacher and asked if that were true. She kind of sputtered, "Yes, no, yes, but no!" What could she say? She made the rules. I spent many hours sitting in the hall outside of her class as the semester progressed, but I didn't care. She thought she was punishing me, but I was thrilled that I didn't have to sit and listen to her.

Here are some rules for making up rules. First, go back to your vision and the organization of your class and think about what behaviors inhibit learning—anticipation is everything. Second, physically set up your class to avoid problems before they get there. Spread the students out as much as you can, and allow for unobtrusive movement in the room. Third, make sure whatever consequence you choose for breaking a rule makes sense, and make sure you're willing to enforce it. Never threaten. Fourth, design a number of activities to help the students develop a sense of community about your class. Students are not as likely to act inappropriately if they feel they are important members of a team with common goals. Finally, spend some time demonstrating to your students why you have the specific rules in place, how the consequences are logical, and what the rewards are. The students should definitely have the idea you have rules in your class, not for some false sense of power, but to simplify things and eliminate chaos. The rules help them.

I mentioned earlier that one of the hardest things about being a teacher is you are a constant role model. When you deal with your students, you show them how to solve problems. You can talk all you want, but they pay attention to what you do. When you yell and scream at a class, do not be surprised when they yell and scream back at you. If you show them no respect, don't be surprised when they show you none. A teacher who controls a class through threats and accusations had better never turn her back. This kind of power is no power at all. All of us can physically make a student do something—we may have to call in a bigger teacher or an administrator—but there's no trick to making a kid shut up and sit down. It's keeping him there that's difficult.

If I want to get out of working in your class, I'll just kick up dust and distract you. That teacher who dragged me to the office so many years ago thought she had won, but actually, I did. I successfully delayed her lesson for at least 20 minutes and made her look like a fool in front of her students and her principal. Sure, she gave me an F—been there, done that. That's one way I can tell which teachers are not very good at what they're doing— they have a high percentage of Fs in their grade books. How hard is that? What's difficult is to have a high percentage of students succeed. Can you think of another business in the world where workers can fail to turn out half their products and keep their jobs? Only in education. Failing a student is not a sign of power, it's an admission of defeat. I do not believe in giving away passing grades; that is also a sign of false power. But over and over I see new, as well as experienced, teachers using grades to punish students. Kids who are really behavior problems probably have a string of Fs on their belts—it means nothing to them. Many of them wear the failing grades with pride and are so out of control at home, your threat doesn't even faze them.

Failing a student
is not a sign of power,
it's an admission
of defeat.

One of our main goals as teachers should be to help students learn self-discipline, and we can't accomplish this if the only control we understand comes from the person in the position of authority. I have a way of making my students understand the true nature of power. I pick the biggest guy in the group and tell him that I can force him to stay in my class. The kids kind of chuckle when I tell the student to try to leave, but it is impossible because I'm between him and the door. I stand behind the kid and push down on his shoulders and tell him in a strained voice, "OK, now try to leave—you can't do it because I'll hold you back." Everyone laughs when the student easily throws off my hands and heads for the door. I act stunned and ask the group what went wrong. They quickly point out that he was bigger and stronger and wanted to leave. I nod and say, "All right, physical force didn't work, let's try something else." This time I sit down next to the boy, tell him that I will spend the next few months doing everything in my power to help him succeed in his goals, that I am really glad he's there, and that I've got all sorts of interesting things to teach him. Then I ask if he'd like to stay. He always says yes, and I point out that no one in the room could force him to leave now because he wants to be there. That is true power and the strongest kind of control.

During the first week of a class, I spend about 20 minutes every day discussing the rules, consequences, and rewards of the class. I have a list of general rules I submit on the assertive discipline form, and these go home to be signed by parents. Right now the five rules in my class are these:

1. Be on time.
2. Come prepared to work and stay on task.
3. Don't disturb other students.
4. No food or drinks allowed in the room.
5. Know why you are doing an assignment.

Do you see how it is possible to enforce "Don't disturb other students" rather than falling into the "No talking" trap? Students talk in class—you want them to. What you don't want is for their talking to disturb others and inhibit the learning process. True, this is a judgment call, but that's why they pay you the big bucks. I have known students who were put in detention because they leaned over and asked their neighbor what page they were on. There's a big difference between this and a kid talking so loud that no one can hear what anyone else is saying. My students don't like the fourth rule about no food or drinks because many teachers allow them to do this. To be honest, if I were in someone's class, I'd like to have the option

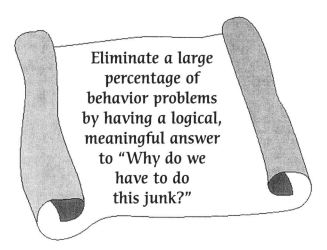

Eliminate a large percentage of behavior problems by having a logical, meaningful answer to "Why do we have to do this junk?"

of having a drink on my desk, and I tell my students that. The reason I've banned these things is because of the computers. Students always swear to me that they will never, never take their drinks anywhere near the computers, but it happens every year. After one student accidentally spilled his soft drink on a keyboard, I called it quits. The students usually accept this because it makes sense, and I also use this rule as a reward sometimes. I have a small refrigerator in my room and if a class is working particularly well for the first few weeks, I give them the privilege of putting their drinks in there. They have to promise to quietly get their drink when they need it, but the drinks can never disturb the groups and must stay in the refrigerator. Because of the four-period day, classes are long, and some kids have a hard time making it to lunch. But they clearly understand that this privilege is mine to give and to take away, and it's up to them to guard it carefully. The fifth rule seems silly, but students who understand why they are doing an assignment not only complete the work but are not likely to give you a problem because they see the point of what you're asking them to do. You can eliminate a large proportion of behavior problems by having a logical, meaningful answer to "Why do we have to do this junk?"

I have another set of about 15 rules that describes specifically what I expect the students to do when we work in groups. These rules include never even giving the appearance of sleeping, not playing games like Solitaire on the computer, and having all their work ready when their group shifts to meet with me. I explain the logic of these rules, and we practice them for several days. I point out how the entire system is designed to ensure that the small group I'm working with gets my undivided attention for the short time I see them every day. The rules benefit the students because one third of the time they are in the special group at my table.

The consequences of breaking the rules in my class are the same for all but being tardy. That's a general school rule, and we follow the schoolwide consequences—three tardies equal one day absent. For all the other rules, I give a verbal warning, quickly and quietly reminding them of what they should be doing. If they ignore the verbal warning, I ask them to copy out the group rules stapled in their folders. This covers about a page of typing and is just annoying enough that they don't want to do it. This written list of rules must be turned in at the beginning of class the next day. If the student does not turn in the list, the write-off is doubled, and if they fail to submit that, they go to detention until the write-off is completed. This series of consequences is fairly logical and easy to enforce.

One of the best ways to eliminate discipline problems is to have a reputation as a good teacher who tries to make learning enjoyable but who will do what she says she is going to do.

What are the rewards for following the rules? Students get to be in my class. I know this sounds conceited, but one of the best ways to eliminate discipline problems is to have a reputation as a good teacher who tries to make learning enjoyable but who will do what she says she is going to do.

When the special education teachers meet with parents and students to plan for next year, they often say if the student is very good, he or she may get to be in Mrs. Gill's class next year. I'm one of the few teachers in the school who doesn't mind working with kids with special needs and who will not make excuses for them. I also inherit many younger brothers, sisters, sweethearts, and friends of former students. They tend to be predisposed to like my class. I don't believe in giving movies or free days as rewards because these have been overused. I tell the students their main rewards are that authentic learning occurs in this class and everything we do is designed to make them successful in the future. You'd be surprised how effective this is.

When I review the rules on the third day, I role play to make sure that everyone understands exactly what happens when we break into groups the following week. From the minute they walk in the class, I carefully check to identify the kids with attitudes or the ones who overtly call attention to themselves. Even though I don't know them yet, these kids are fairly easy to spot. I tell the students that we're going to go over the rules and consequences one more time to make sure there are no misunderstandings. Then I innocently pick one of the potential troublemakers, and say, "Let's say it's next week and everyone is in groups, working away. I'm up at the board getting ready to work with my group. I turn around and (gasp) Joe is sitting there talking with Julie! He's supposed to be on the computers! I'm stunned, but I figure he just lost track of the time. I say, 'Joe, you need to get on the computers,' and naturally he smiles, gives me a nod, and gets right to work. He's a great guy. But let's pretend, and I know that this would never happen, but let's pretend that Joe is just having a really bad day and I look up again, and he's *still* sitting there talking to Julie. I can barely believe my eyes I'm so shocked. I say, 'Joe, you need to copy out the group rules stapled in your folder.' I figure he just forgot what he was supposed to do and it will help him out."

Then, I turn to the class in general and ask, "When I give Joe the write-off, what does he say?" This usually causes general snickers because Joe probably has a history of fighting with teachers, but I break in and say, "Joe says, 'Thank you, Mrs. Gill, thank you for giving me this write-off, because you told me that if I ignored your verbal warning, that's what would happen. I even signed a paper agreeing to it, so I want to thank you for being the kind of person who does what she says she's going to do—the kind of person I can trust—bless your heart!'" By now the class is howling, including Joe, but the point is made. There's no arguing when a teacher asks a student to fulfill the consequence of breaking a rule because the student agreed to it ahead of time to stay in the class, and the teacher said that this is what she would do.

The next day, we role-play again using a different student, and we practice doubling the write-off and heading on down to detention. Again, I point out that the student will probably be thanking me profusely as we walk down the hall to the office because I'm the kind of person who keeps her word. At the end of the week, they take a quiz on the rules, and this is the first grade of the semester. Most students get a perfect score, which lets me know that they understand completely what I expect. When I hand back the tests, I can clear up any confusion, and by the time we break into groups the following week, the class runs pretty smoothly.

Just as I don't mind stopping at a traffic light, most students understand that rules are designed to protect them and to create an optimum learning environment.

I rarely take a student to the office—once a year at the most. When I do, the student is in some serious trouble, because it's such a rare occurrence. There are teachers in my school who average one student to the principal per class period. I'm not sure if they do this to scare the students or to get out of embarrassing situations, but it's a huge mistake. It sends two negative messages to two very important groups of people. One, it gives administrators the impression the teacher cannot handle the students. Two, it lets the students know the teacher is not the bottom line; it's the administrators who count. I handle almost all my disciplinary problems myself—the students know it's between the two of us and it will be solved. I do ask advice from counselors and other teachers to find out background information that may give me clues as to why students are acting up in class.

When creating a discipline plan for your class, do the following:

1. Anticipate possible problems ahead of time.

2. Create an internal system allowing students to control most of their own behavior.

3. Be sure your rules are logical and can be enforced.

4. Spend quite a bit of time reviewing the rules and consequences so there is no doubt in anyone's mind about what you expect.

5. Do what you say you will do every time in as matter-of-fact a manner as possible.

Just as I don't mind stopping at a traffic light, most students understand that rules are designed to protect them and to create an optimum learning environment. The sixth commandment of good teaching? Thou shalt be fair and prepared for problems before they get there.

Thou Shalt Use Some Common Sense

I've spent a great deal of time telling you about the very specific set of rules and consequences I've designed for my class. I have to run a pretty tight ship because of the small amount of time I have to teach each of the groups. However, teaching is a people business and stuff happens. There are times when you have to make a judgment call based on old-fashioned common sense. There's always an exception to every rule, and you have to be able to read a situation quickly enough to defuse it before gets out of hand. By working with your students as individually as possible, you can get fairly adept at separating the reliable kids from the players.

There are very few times I allow a student to sit and do nothing in my class. The kids just know they have to work all period long because that's what I expect. But occasionally, a student comes in who is obviously agitated and at the breaking point. Something may have happened at home or in the last class, and this kid is ready to blow. If I see this, I'll sit next to him or her while the other students move around getting into the groups. I'll try to get the troubled student to tell me what is wrong, but sometimes he or she won't talk or—even worse—the student will scream at me. Right then I have to make a decision. I hope I know enough about this student to guess what's wrong. Based on my instincts, I'll take the student into the hall to talk, take the student to the office to talk to someone else, or leave him or her alone to cool down. The one thing I know I *won't* do is take the anger personally. This child may scream that he or she hates me, but unless I've done something on purpose to make this kid mad, I'm not going to react to the words. This is just misplaced rage, and I'd be a fool to buy into it by losing my temper, too.

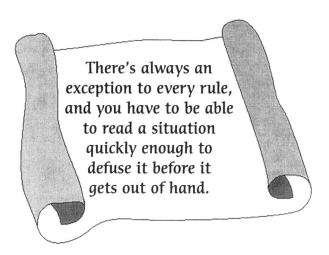

There's always an exception to every rule, and you have to be able to read a situation quickly enough to defuse it before it gets out of hand.

Remember, the teacher is the role model. I'm not going to show the students just the same amount of respect they show me, because I'm the adult. I'll actually show them far more respect, so they may learn by example. Sometimes students tell me I give them too much work or they don't feel like doing anything. I could tell them to sit down and shut up or I'll flunk them. I guess that's one solution. But I usually say, "I give you a lot of work because I care about you. If I didn't respect you, I'd let you sit there and do nothing." I'm the one who sets the tone for the class and treats them better than I expect to be treated.

Another tool in my arsenal is a fine-tuned crap detector. I describe this to the students as a little alarm inside me that goes off when I hear something that doesn't add up. I tell them this is one of the most powerful resources they can develop to help them in just about any situation they're likely to encounter. As the semester progresses, I'll call a group up to work with me and someone won't have work done. This person begins an elaborate story about dogs and homework and a best friend's abandoned car. I'll listen politely, then toward the end I'll look startled and say, "Did you hear that?" The kids start looking around. I'll turn my head toward the student and say, "Yep, beep, beep, beep, my crap detector just went off." Usually, everyone starts laughing, including the kid with the excuses. A few years ago, one of my students gave me a headline he'd torn from the newspaper. It said "The Best Crap Detector in the USA." I proudly pasted it to the front of my roll book and sometimes all I need to do is hold it up and point to it.

Another book I find very useful is *Games Students Play* by Ken Ernst (1972). Many students have developed some clever games over the years to outwit teachers. I know I was a major player in high school. One I see all the time is called "Uproar." It goes like this. A student demands to leave the room at an inappropriate time to go to the restroom. The teacher tells the student no. The student goes berserk, screaming and yelling and creating such a fuss that the teacher lets him or her go just to get the student out of the room. Even if the student is not allowed to leave, the teacher makes a mental note that this kid can create quite an uproar. The next time the student makes an unreasonable demand, the teacher gives in to avoid the scene that's sure to follow. This is probably how that student has been training teachers for years. If you spot an Uproar player, never confront him or her in front of the whole class. Make one of those quick decisions either to ignore it right then or to take the student into the hallway. When you get the student alone, call him or her on the game. Tell the student without a trace of anger in your voice you didn't realize that he or she was an Uproar player and you're glad you found out. Smile, nod knowingly, and say you recognize this is how the student has controlled teachers for years, but luckily for him or her, you are a teacher who understands this game and won't play. Quickly explain why you wouldn't let the student leave the class and how you'd like to handle the same situation in the future. Before you return to class, tell the student you're glad he or she is there, but because you have so much to accomplish, you just can't have any outbursts like that. This may sound naive to you, but it really works. Remember to handle all discipline problems as matter-of-factly as possible.

Because you're learning to anticipate problems before they occur, you need to develop a simple system allowing students to leave your class to use the restroom. This may sound ridiculous, but I've noticed this becomes one of the biggest fights bringing an angry teacher and an angrier student to the principal's office. Refusing to allow students to use the restroom during a 90-minute class is setting yourself up for some serious battles—with parents as well as students. It is almost impossible to tell whether a student really has to go, so don't even play that game. I taught for a year next door to a new teacher who was having a horrible time making his students behave. I could literally hear desks being thrown against the wall, and I went over a couple of times, but it embarrassed the teacher so much that I stopped doing it. I offered to help in any way I could, but the teacher was afraid to let anyone know how much trouble he was having because he thought he could lose his job as a result. He was fired anyway. In a desperate attempt to control his students, he forbade anyone to leave the class under any circumstances. In his defense, he had students leaving four and five times within an hour to "use the bathroom." He told them they had abused the privilege, so he was taking it away. I was horrified to learn later in the year that one student had urinated in the corner of the room because he said he couldn't hold it any longer. This shows how uncontrollable things can get when a teacher creates a rule that can't be enforced.

Many of your students will have developed some pretty clever games over the years to outwit teachers.

In my class, the students are free to leave the class once per period. I don't ask them where they're going, but they know they have to follow the regular school rules. I leave the hall pass on a counter by the door. They have to sign out, stating where they're going, when they left, and when they returned. I tell them that they cannot leave when their small group is working with me. The only other requirement is that they enter and exit so quietly that no one notices. If they cause a disturbance, they forfeit the privilege for a week. It works fairly smoothly, and it's rare that a student abuses the system. The best advice I can give is to pick and choose your fights. Arguing about whether the students legitimately need to use the restroom is not one I choose to take on.

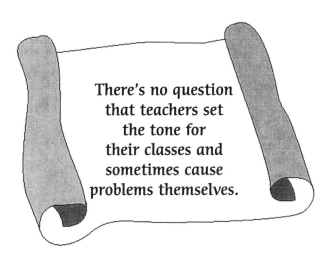

There's no question that teachers set the tone for their classes and sometimes cause problems themselves.

It's been my experience that people have a great deal of control over how others react to them. There's no question that teachers set the tone for their classes and sometimes cause problems themselves. Many years ago, I read *Transactional Analysis in Psychotherapy* by Eric Berne (1961), the author of *Games People Play*. In this book, Berne describes a system of behavioral modification called transactional analysis (TA). I found this especially helpful in developing my instincts for dealing with students. In fact, I teach a mini-unit in TA to my students because it's so useful in explaining why people respond to us so differently. According to TA, each of us has learned how to be a parent, an adult, and a child by observing the behavior of the significant people in our lives. I tell my students that from the moment they are born, a little tape recorder goes on in their heads. We record on these tapes, without evaluating, what it is to be a parent by watching our parents, what it is to be an adult by watching the few we run into, and we experience naturally what it is to be a child. We all have a part of us that reacts like a Critical Parent, a Nurturing Parent, an Adult, a

Submissive Child, a Rebellious Child, and a Free Child. Depending on the personalities of the significant role models in our lives, we may have more of one than another. For example, a student who was abandoned or poorly cared for as a child does not react very often in a Nurturing Parent manner because that's just not something he or she learned while growing up. Someone who grew up under the thumb of a Critical Parent either learned to be submissive to survive or possibly fought back in a rebellious manner. That person tends to act in the same critical manner as a parent.

Frustrated, embarrassed students will usually become behavior problems.

I try to get students to analyze themselves and focus on how they most often react to other people. I also point out that many of the "transactional states" are symbiotic. A Nurturing Parent loves to deal with a Submissive Child. Think how this works in a classroom. Teachers who choose to control their students through threats and constant put-downs, the modus operandi of the Critical Parent, naturally recognize and respond negatively to the Rebellious Child in many of their students. Ultimately, the teacher is the one who fuels the conflict by not understanding what is going on. There is no way I'm going to get into a head-on confrontation with a Rebellious Child. I may win a few battles, but I'll surely lose the war. In the same manner, I'm not about to stay in my Nurturing Parent when dealing with my students. Even though this may bring out their submissive natures, it also makes them dependent on me and therefore, they remain in a childlike state. The logical place to stay in most of our relationships at school is in our Adults. This is the part of us that makes decisions based on the best information available. It tends to bring out the Adult in the students. I would encourage anyone who deals with people on a regular basis to read Berne's book. It was one of those trendy philosophies that sweep through the schools on a regular basis that has actually worked for me for many, many years.

Sometimes it seems to me that most of the people who become educators were also the top students in their schools. They were the kids the teachers loved because they were so quiet and well mannered and always had their work done on time. Some of these students go on to become remarkable teachers. However, I've noticed that teachers who never had to struggle to learn or to control their behavior tend to have very little tolerance for the students who do. We may have loved math when we were young, but there are students who find it so baffling and frustrating that they do whatever they can to keep the teacher from talking about it. As teachers, we have to be sensitive to the fact that few of our students learn in the same manner as we do, and we have to learn to accommodate these differences. Frustrated, embarrassed students will usually become behavior problems. You need to develop a set of rules by which to run your classes, but sometimes you are called on to make decisions based on your instincts rather than the normal solutions. The seventh commandment of good teaching? When making choices that affect your students, thou shalt use some common sense.

Thou Shalt Be Open-Minded and Flexible

Teachers are natural-born leaders. They have to be. But this is why most faculty meetings are such unpleasant experiences. It isn't just staying after school for an extra couple of hours; it's that the room is full of highly opinionated, pushy people who are used to telling others what to do. In all human beings, the quality that is our greatest strength can also be our greatest weakness. There is a fine line between being decisive and being overbearing; between being in charge and being a martinet. When the bell rings and the door closes to the classroom, we're the boss. One of my favorite things about teaching is that no one is looking over my shoulder telling me what to do. The quality of what goes on in my classroom is solely in my hands.

However, I don't teach in isolation. I am part of a community of teachers, and I'm responsible for that group as well. I constantly wrestle with the impulse to stay in my room and ignore the rest of the world. Sometimes I'll pass a classroom where the students are obviously out of control and the teacher is struggling. What I most want to do is turn my head and move on. But at my best, I realize that all the students in the school are my students and I have an obligation to at least offer to help.

Teaching can be the loneliest profession in the world. When I first began teaching in a middle school in Tennessee, the principal handed me a roll book, a key to my room, and wished me luck. I didn't even know how to take roll and that teachers would be expected to buy most of their supplies, such as chalk. Except for one advanced English class, I struggled through that year, and no one on the staff paid any attention. I was too embarrassed to admit I was having problems because I thought that would make me appear incompetent. My family had just moved to the area from California, and I didn't know a soul. It was the closest I've come to quitting the profession. I had a terrible year because no one offered to help and I didn't ask. Most of the teachers I know have had similar experiences and tend to be very nice about looking out for a newcomer.

I am part of a community of teachers, and I'm responsible for that group as well. I constantly wrestle with the impulse to stay in my room.

On the other hand, keep in mind that teachers are also an opinionated lot who offer advice even when it isn't requested. One of the main things I try to remember when I attempt to help someone is that we do not all teach in the same way. Schools are filled with all types of personalities and styles. I think I do a good job in my classes, but I have had students who I feel gained little from being in my class. Either they couldn't handle the freedom inherent in my system or they found my earnestness obnoxious. They responded far better to a teacher who sat the students in rows and lectured for most of the period. We all have different teaching and learning styles, and we should honor those. The bottom line is whether your style accomplishes your goals.

One of the biggest traps a teacher can fall into is to spend even a small amount of time worrying or griping about what teachers down the hall are or aren't doing. First, unless they request your input, it's none of your business. However, if their classes are so chaotic they disturb your class, that's a different story. The first step is to speak to the individual teachers, explain the problem, and offer any assistance you can. The second step is to talk to an administrator about the problem. But this should occur only if what other teachers are doing interferes with what you are trying to do.

I have been asked to serve on our Faculty Advisory Committee for years, but I usually refuse. This committee is chosen by the other faculty members to present their concerns to the principal in regular monthly meetings. The idea behind it is to save time, and it also allows a teacher to bring up a sensitive issue anonymously. I used to think this committee was a powerful force to help steer the school toward a collective vision. In reality, meetings were usually rather lengthy gripe sessions. Members took turns presenting lists of suggestions from the faculty at large. Ninety percent of these suggestions were either complaints about another faculty member or gripes about situations that were unsolvable because of budget constraints. Very few were suggestions or solutions. I stopped participating in this process when I realized no one was really interested in seeking a solution—it was just a lot of negative energy harmful to the morale of the school.

Earlier in this book, I encouraged you to ask when you need something, but be careful what you ask for because you might get it. For example, some teachers in my school spend an inordinate amount of time worrying about what other teachers wear to school. At one point, they demanded the principal do something about the "unprofessional" colleagues, so the principal offered to set up a very rigid dress code for all teachers. These same teachers were outraged—they didn't want someone dictating what they could or couldn't wear. They primarily wanted to complain. Years ago, I heard a story about a two-year-old boy, sucking on a pacifier, who was sitting next to his mother. The mother was talking with a large group of women who were planning a party. One of the women kept staring at the boy and finally said, "What in the world are you doing sucking on that pacifier, a big boy like you? That's for babies." The little boy took the pacifier out of his mouth, looked the woman straight in the eye, and said, "Hurts you?" I can't tell you how often this saying runs through my head when I'm listening to teachers complain about one another. I want to ask, "Hurts you?"

We have to learn
to pick and choose
our battles.

Every year we have a summer faculty meeting during which we discuss plans for the following school year. Every year someone brings up the sorry state of student dress and demands a strictly enforced dress code. This usually results in an hour-long debate over the finer issues such as how baggy can pants be before they're outlawed? How short is too short for a skirt or top? The trouble is that most of these teachers can't define their terms. When I first moved here, I was surprised to hear that boys were not allowed to wear tank tops, but girls were. In my first faculty meeting, I naively asked what was wrong with tank tops and was told that some of the teachers just couldn't stand to see underarm hair. I didn't know how to respond to that; it seemed so ridiculous. We have to learn to pick and choose our battles, and a student dress code is one that screams for common sense. The other teachers know that I pay very little attention to what my students wear because I'm looking so hard at their faces to make sure they understand what I'm saying. They'd have to have on something pretty outrageous for me to notice.

This debate has gone on so long that when the dress code issue is brought up in a meeting, everyone turns to hear me declare my ultraradical, bleeding-heart opposition to strict rules dictating how the kids dress. But what I say year after year seems to be such common sense to me. If what a student is wearing interferes with the learning environment, send that student out of class to change. For that matter, if what a teacher is wearing interferes with the learning environment, that teacher should change. That's it. Sure this requires judgment calls, but that's why we're the highly respected professionals we're paid to be. I personally would never even notice whether students have on hats in my class unless the brim covers their eyes. If that is the case, I tell them to take the hats off. This is not a big problem. But I have known teachers to waste half a class period in the office with a student who may or may not have on baggy pants. One of the most disgusting scenes I've observed as a teacher was two male administrators on their knees in front of a 16-year-old girl measuring the length of her skirt. A girl's skirt is too short if it is so distracting that the other students or the teacher cannot concentrate in class.

As we get older, we tend to conveniently forget what we were like when we were young. Every one of us wore or wanted to wear something that was against the authority figure's rules. Teens are dominated by fads, and the way they dress is an attempt to illustrate to the world who they think they are. I don't advocate allowing students to wear gang colors or anything that could harm anyone. One of our main goals in a school is to provide a safe learning environment, and we must react swiftly and decisively when it comes to protecting our students. But we also need to remember that the vast majority of the kids in our schools are pretty reasonable, good people. Just as it's a huge mistake to punish an entire class for the misdeeds of a few, it's wrong to force all the students to follow rules set up to punish a few bad seeds. We have to be a little open-minded about people who dress and act differently from ourselves. People should be judged by their actions, not their appearances. People should be judged by the end result, not necessarily by how they got there.

Remember that the vast majority of the kids in our schools are pretty reasonable, good people.

We're in a people business, and we have to remain flexible to survive. Another of my favorite things about teaching is that every 90 minutes everything changes. A whole new set of students comes in with a variety of social, religious, racial, and political backgrounds. If teachers become bored with their jobs, it may be because they've focused so hard on teaching a subject, they've forgotten that they're really teaching students. Not too long ago, a student in one of my classes was killed in a car accident. Former students of mine have died before, but never while they were members of my class. The young man was killed because he and his friend had been drinking. He was by no means a top student; Joe had been involved in gangs and had just returned from the alternative school because he'd been caught smoking on campus so many times. He had a learning disability and an extremely short fuse. To top it off, he was hyperactive, which had caused some real headaches for many teachers. But in my experience, he was kind-hearted, funny, and great with computers. He and I got along because he knew I liked him, and I would not allow him to behave inappropriately in class.

They kept Joe on a life support system for two days after the accident. As I was leaving school that Monday, the office secretary called to let me know Joe had died. I knew the next day would be difficult not only because I felt terrible, but because I knew many of his friends would be upset as well. On Tuesday morning, one of our counselors announced over the PA system Joe had died and asked us to think about him during the moment of silence that begins every school day. This brought a few tears to my eyes, but I started to lose it when a senior who had been in a gang with Joe came into my room, threw his arms around me, and started crying. I took him out into the hall and we both cried a little out there. I calmed him down, sent him back to class, and headed to the front office to wash my face. Halfway there, one of the male teachers asked me to go into the girls' restroom because he could hear screeching and loud noises. I found nine girls, some lying on the floor, crying their eyes out. I sat down and tried to talk to them a bit, but they were extremely upset and more girls were joining them. Finally, I asked them to come sit with me in the cafeteria so we wouldn't block the door. By then I was surrounded by about 20 girls and boys, most of whom were crying. I sat next to one girl who was just about hysterical and rubbed her back and talked to her. Just when I had them calmed down, one of the administrators came by and asked what we were doing. I told her that these students had been friends of Joe and needed someone to talk to. She said that unfortunately, these things do happen, but it was best just to stay busy and not dwell on them. Then she ordered every-one back to class. I had to physically restrain one girl from attacking her. I told the administrator as calmly as I could that I would sit with these students for a while, but that she needed to send someone from the front office to talk with them. She pressed her lips together and marched off. No one came, even after I sent two other people to ask for help. Finally, I took the group, which had swollen to about 30 students, back to my room. I had a first-period class, I was in the middle of preparing my seniors to write their research papers, and I didn't want to spend my day trying to talk with these kids who weren't even my students. But I also had to be flexible enough to realize that this was an extraordinary situation, and the best lesson I could teach that day was compassion.

Period after period, students filed into my room to sit and cry or mourn. During that day, I was able to talk to gang members and students who were abusing alcohol and drugs about the likely consequences of their choices. The administrators had presented a program at the last teachers' meeting about gangs, and we had discussed ways to keep gangs from polluting our school. But not one administrator came down to my room to talk to these kids. They were there—the gang members—and they were in a vulnerable state. The door was open, and no one came. True, these were some of the worst kids in the school. True, they were supposed to be in class, and they were breaking the rules by coming to my room. True, this one incident would probably not change everything, but it could change some things.

I love teaching because of the combination of left-brain linear, logical work and right-brain creative, intuitive work.

We have all heard of the "teachable moment," that magic time when what you say is exactly what the student needs (and is ready) to hear. It doesn't happen all the time, but as a teacher, you have to be flexible enough to grab it. I love teaching because of the combination of left-brain linear, logical work and right-brain creative, intuitive work. As a songwriter, my husband understands this miracle. Often he'll work on a song for several months, fine-tuning it or even changing it completely. But every once in a while, a song drops into his lap finished, and he has to scramble to get it written down before it goes away. I call this the funnel to heaven, and I believe gifted people can access this.

Sometimes a lesson I've prepared about writing business letters evolves into a life-altering experience. Chuck was a student in senior English who came with a warning sticker practically stamped on his forehead. He was an infamous troublemaker with a volatile temper. He and I understood each other, and I was able to teach him a great deal about word processors and writing. Whenever I teach business letters, I point out how powerful they are as problem-solving tools. I show examples of letters I've written, and I talk about what the letters accomplished. One day, I was sitting in my room during my planning period and the door slammed open. Chuck burst in, and I could see immediately he was about to explode. He asked me if he could use one of my computers, and I said, "OK, but don't break it." I could tell he didn't want to talk, so I worked at my desk while he typed away. After much mumbling, he brought a beautifully crafted business letter to my desk for me to read. It turned out he'd been accused of doing something, not because of any proof, but because of his reputation. He asked me to show him how to change the format so he could address the letter to all school board members and the superintendent of schools. I was stunned. This was a kid who normally would have slashed the principal's tires or torn down the paper-towel holders in the bathrooms. Now he was using something I'd taught him to solve a problem in an adult manner. I couldn't have been more proud.

In another senior English class, I had a group of "skaters" who were constantly clashing with teachers and administrators about the dress code. Teachers would grab them in the hall and yank up their pants or pull off their wallet chains. The students had very little respect for authority figures, and most were in school only because they'd lose their driver's licenses if they quit. They were a real challenge to teach. As luck would have it, the administrators sent out a lengthy memo outlining a new, rather strict dress code and asked all teachers to read it to their classes. This caused general outrage among the students, even those who would never dream of wearing anything out of the ordinary to school, because of the dictatorial nature of the mandate. I overheard one of the leaders of the skaters planning some mayhem for after school. I quietly joined the group and complimented them for playing right into the administrators' hands. They looked at me suspiciously as I told them causing some destruction to the school would be the best way possible for the administrators to justify their strict rules. The administrators could then say, "See, these kids are out of hand and we have to crack down on them!"

Michael, the leader, asked me if I thought they should just roll over and take it. I told him both solutions he'd suggested—senseless violence or passivity—sounded pretty chicken to me. He bristled all over and asked me what I thought they should do. I asked the group to tell me whether they were really interested in challenging the dress code or if they just wanted to be a rebel like everyone else. I also asked them if they were willing to put in the extra time and attention a real solution would require. They assured me they were serious and tired of being pushed around. So I altered my lesson plans right there and created a unit to show them how to be proactive rather than reactive.

Because we work with people, we have to be ready to embrace the unexpected and make it work.

Talk about student motivation. This group of 10 kids who rarely worked in any class became a dynamic organization. They started by interviewing the administrators to get the facts behind the new rules. Then the students developed a questionnaire to poll other students and teachers about their attitudes toward the dress code. Next, the students drafted a report summarizing all of the results and offering suggestions for a compromise. Finally, we invited the principal to class, at which time Michael orally presented the highlights of the report. When he left, the principal had a professional-looking, 20-page report and a new vision of these kids. He didn't throw out the dress code, but he did make modifications. My students were exhilarated by the experience, and all 10 went on to graduate.

When I started teaching at this rural Tennessee high school, I was assigned to teach vocational English. The vocational director was an older man, who was also a farmer on the side. He didn't know what to think of this crazy woman from California who spoke and acted so differently from everyone else. He viewed all of us foreigners with suspicion, and although he was nice, he kept me at arm's length. One day, I came to him with a proposal for a project I wanted to try with my students. He hemmed and hawed and didn't know how to respond. Finally I said, "You know, if we combine some Tennessee 'know-how' with some California 'why not,' we could create the best vocational English program in the state." He loved that idea, and he helped me get my first computers. Some of my colleagues think I'm a laid-back, leftover flower child because I do unusual things in my classes and I stand up for the rights of students. Actually, if they ever watched me teach, they'd see that I'm organized to a fault and tolerate very few inappropriate behaviors. I just understand that because we work with people, we have to be ready to embrace the unexpected and make it work. The eighth commandment of good teaching? Thou shalt be open-minded and flexible to be successful; you have no other choice.

Thou Shalt Not Work in Fear

My entire teaching career has been a series of successes and failures. The successes have given me the confidence and the reputation that have earned me the freedom I enjoy. But my own best teacher has always been failure. A sign that hangs above the computers in my room says, "People who never make mistakes work for people who aren't afraid to." I've made about every mistake in the book, but each one has helped me refine my program, allowing me to rewrite a rule or throw out a lesson and add another. After teaching for six years, I decided to put a couch in my classroom so my students could be comfortable when they were reading. It's a struggle to get some of my students to even open a book; therefore, I'm constantly searching for ways to help them associate reading with pleasure. It seemed like a great idea, but even with the best of intentions, students would nod off with a book on their chests. They would also fight over who got to sit on the couch, and I finally decided the couch was causing more problems than it was worth. I went back to a table and chairs the following year.

You can't expect your first year of teaching to be stress free, and you certainly shouldn't give up just because there were problems. You can allow the problems to defeat you or you can analyze what worked, give yourself credit for what went well, and change what didn't. You need to take chances every year, because if you try to please everyone, you'll end up pleasing no one, especially yourself.

Successes have given me the confidence and the reputation that have earned me the freedom I enjoy. But my own best teacher has always been failure.

I've had teachers sit in my class watching every move I make, and then try to teach exactly as I do. It never works. You have to create your own style, your own program, and build enough confidence in it to help you weather the inevitable criticism. There is never a point in time when everyone is thrilled with what you're doing—it's not possible. I used to moan and groan over the one or two students each year who really hated my class. After listening to this for a while, my husband finally asked, "How about the 98% who loved what you did?" That really helped me to shift my focus from the failures to the successes. A person who pleases everyone is probably teaching within such safe borders, there is no room for growth.

Watch everyone, learn from everyone, but follow your instincts. When designing my classes, I knew I could never live with total quiet or total chaos, so I found a place somewhere between the two that matches my rhythms. Teachers are often guilty of criticizing a colleague who teaches in a different style just because it's not how they would do it. Schools would be pretty dull places if everyone taught and learned in exactly the same manner. My daughters have two favorite teachers in common. One was a strict disciplinarian who lectured 95% of the time; the other was a child-centered person who encouraged creativity and risk. The girls loved both of them. These teachers had found their own styles, which freed them to communicate their love for their subjects, and that's all that mattered. Leave yourself open to all suggestions, but use your instincts and experiences to filter out the ones that don't work for you.

To be successful as a teacher, you have to understand the balance of power in the system. When I'm teaching my seniors about succeeding in their chosen careers, I ask them to draw a chart showing the balance of power in our school district. I tell them to place the most important people on top and the least important at the bottom. It amazes me that year after year the kids put the superintendent at the top and the students at the bottom. They're shocked when I tell them that they have it all wrong. They need to turn their charts upside down to view them correctly. The most important people in our school systems are the students and their parents. They pay our salaries through taxes, and we work for them. The seniors love it when I place the teachers right under the students and often decide to fire someone before the end of the day. One of my favorite responses when students ask, "Why do you make us do so much work?" is "Because that's what you hired me to do. Do you want me to waste your money?" Below the teachers on my version of this chart come the counselors and support personnel. Next are the administrators, and finally, we add the superintendent and school board. You may think I'm being facetious, but think about the logic here. The principal's job is to clear the way for me to teach. He works for me in that he removes anything that keeps me from doing the best job I can. The superintendent works for the principal in the same manner. She provides whatever is required to make the principal successful in his job. This may seem topsy-turvy at first, but without students, we have no job. We're the only employees in the world who can have dissatisfied customers and keep our jobs. The government is continually threatening to create vouchers that will make everyone view the balance of power in the schools in a different way. Tenure may become a thing of the past.

When you begin teaching in a school, you'd be wise to uncover where the true power lies. Many new teachers live in terror of their principals or supervisors, but administrators are not necessarily the most influential people in a school. During the lesson on the balance of power, I ask my students to name the two people in the school for whom I'll do anything—the two people I most want to keep happy because they can make or break my job. The kids are always surprised when I identify the two people I need the most as the bookkeeper and the head maintenance man. I have found these two to be the bottom-line experts on almost every project I've tried to get off the ground. Sometimes I'll see teachers or administrators treat janitors, maintenance personnel, and secretaries like poor relations; that is a huge mistake. If angered, these people can cause you more trouble than any principal could hope to do.

I'll give you an example. The head of maintenance for my school has worked there since it opened. He moves slowly and doesn't say much. He has little formal education, and some teachers treat him as they would a servant when they demand his services. The mistake they make is in underestimating his intelligence and not noticing the twinkle in his eye. I've seen him stand calmly while an irate teacher chewed him out about something broken in her classroom. The teacher usually finishes by saying she wants the problem taken care of immediately! Mr. P. just stands there and waits for her to finish. Then he tells her he will file the necessary forms right away. First, he'll submit the forms to the secretary, who'll get the principal's approval. Then the forms are sent to the central office, where they are processed and returned to him. He hopes, he tells the teacher, to get the forms back before the end of the week. Then he walks off with that twinkle in his eye. The truth is Mr. P. runs the school and can fix anything he chooses when he chooses. The teacher is a fool not to understand how important Mr. P. is and to give him the respect he deserves.

The kids are always surprised when I identify the two people I need the most as the bookkeeper and the head maintenance man.

The best way to survive all of the nonsense and politics occurring in any business is to find your people, do everything you can to keep them happy, and operate through them. One of my best friends in my school is a technology teacher. He and I think very much alike, and we both make it our business to ensure the other's success. My classroom used to be directly above Steve's, and he used that to my advantage. We had a supervisor from the central office who dropped by the schools every so often, not to encourage and support what was going well, but to sniff out what was wrong. Steve and I would amuse ourselves by driving this man crazy. For example, if Steve noticed that the supervisor had entered the building, he'd flip on a rarely used band saw that let everyone in the area know that a negative force was on the loose. We never really had anything to hide, but it was fun.

> The best way to survive all of the nonsense and politics that occur in any business is to find your people, do everything you can to keep them happy, and operate through them.

One time this supervisor came to my room to observe me. He was armed with about 20 very detailed forms that, when passed through an elaborate scoring system, would tell him whether I was doing a good job or not. He was a big supporter of the state model for teaching, which specifically timed a teacher as he or she moved through the narrow confines of their idea of the ideal lesson plan. When I saw what he was doing, I told him I was glad that beginning or poor teachers had such a model to help them out, but that he'd be crazy to ask someone like me to alter a program that had proved to be successful. He became rather agitated, but when he added up all the numbers, I was one point away from a perfect score. You have no idea how angry that made him. I taught in a completely different style from that in which he had been trained, but it still worked.

There are always people similar to this rigid supervisor in your life, and you have to choose how much control to give them. You already know that I'm not afraid of authority figures, but over the years, I have learned when to shut up. There are things that go on in school every day that could upset me; I've just gotten better at picking and choosing my battles.

This was a hard lesson I learned when I first started teaching. I was hired to teach reading and English at a high school in central California. Being the new kid on the block, I was assigned to a portable classroom. When I went in to set it up, I discovered that I had only half the number of desks I needed. I went to the front office, straightforwardly introduced myself to the vice-principal, and told him I needed 12 desks right away. To my surprise, his face closed up, and he said, "We have many teachers who need many things; I'll put your request on a list, but you may just need to make do." I was stunned and embarrassed because what I wanted seemed so reasonable. As I left his office, it occurred to me that it wasn't my request that was hard to take, it was my manner. I was a young woman with a lot of confidence, but he had perceived me as a pushy female. I waited a few hours, and then I returned to his office. This time I acted contrite and confused and told him I really needed his help because I was so nervous about my first job and could he please help out poor, pathetic me. I had the desks within 30 minutes. I felt horrible that I had played the "helpless female" to get what I wanted, but I also learned that the desks were more important than forcing him to treat me with respect. That came later.

If someone is doing something to harm a student, physically or emotionally, I fight that battle. If someone is simply being annoying, I just ignore him. Often students come into my class ready to kill someone because that person had said something they didn't like. My advice is that unless this person is threatening bodily harm to them or their loved ones, don't pay any attention. Students find this very difficult to do, so I offer them my favorite trick. When a person is being ridiculous, yelling at me about a problem I don't own, I visualize him or her as a yappy dog. This allows me to listen and nod, but get no more emotionally involved than I would with a terrier at my ankles. It is completely my choice whether I let this person ruin my day.

It is completely
my choice whether
I let this person
ruin my day.

Most of what goes on outside your classroom is not worthy of your attention, but there are fights you can't be afraid to take on. One year, the principal in my school decided to eradicate drugs from the high school by strip-searching selected students. A surprise announcement came over the PA system instructing us to allow no one to leave classrooms until further notice. We were to wait until a messenger came to our doors to escort certain students to the front office where male and female police officers were waiting. I have always abhorred this reactionary method of controlling drug abuse, but I did what I could to calm my students by pointing out that if they were innocent, they had nothing to worry about. I stood out in the hallway watching the administrators pull students out of classes. Suddenly, I noticed the only students taken to the office were the "hoods" or those from poor families. Without exception, all the males had long hair and all of the females were dressed in leather or "biker" clothes. I asked another teacher to watch my class, and I ran to the office to find the principal. I asked him to tell me what criteria were used to select these students. He told me not to get involved, that he knew who the druggies were, and to go back to class. I pointed out that just because students had long hair or didn't look like his idea of "clean-cut," that didn't automatically mean they were using drugs. I told him if he were really interested in finding the drug abusers, he should pull in a few athletes or some of the rich kids who had the money to spend. He ordered me back to class, and I told him I hoped he would publish the results of this search so we could all see its effectiveness.

Later that day, I was in my room by myself, and one of the kids who had been taken to the office came in. Carl was a tough kid from an extremely poor family. In fact, his mother had died, and his father bothered to check on his children only every once in a while. Carl had a foul mouth, was overtly racist, and rarely wore clean clothes. He was constantly in fights at school because of his inability to accept any point of view other than his own. I had been trying for months to get him to see how the racist attitudes his father had taught him were simply a pathetic attempt to make someone at the bottom rung of society's ladder feel superior to someone else. I'd had little luck, and I sure didn't think the current tension in the room could turn into a teachable moment. He stormed over to me and leaned against the counter where I was working. He avoided my eyes, but I could see he'd been crying. I asked him what had happened and he almost started crying again. "Mrs. Gill, they strip-searched me—they didn't find nothin' because I don't do drugs. I told them that but they didn't care." He slammed his fist against the counter and I told him how sorry I was. The anger was spilling out of him. "They didn't care who I was; I ain't got the money to dress like no rich kid so they just assumed I was guilty." I told him only foolish or scared people judge others by their appearance. He sputtered, "They just look down on my daddy but I'll get my daddy to come down here and kill 'em all. They don't know nothing about me!" At this point, I said that he must be feeling the same kind of frustration a black person feels when all anyone can see is the color of his skin. Carl looked at me shocked, and for just a moment I saw a shift in his eyes, but it was gone as quickly as it appeared. I spent the next 10 minutes trying to calm Carl down, but I know that for just a moment he knew that the stupid way the administrators handled him matched the ignorance he'd shown toward blacks for years. By the way, after humiliating more than 90 students with a strip-search, the administrators found two marijuana seeds in the borrowed jacket of one of the students.

Recently, a new principal ordered a similar lockdown of the entire school, brought in dogs, and searched the purses, backpacks, and pockets of each of the 1,350 students in our school. This time they confiscated aspirin, Midol, cigarettes, lighters, vitamins, and pocketknives. They found no illegal drugs or weapons. We published the results of the search in the school newspaper.

Yes, for reasons that still elude me, my former principal and the English department chairperson signed me up to teach journalism. I had never even taken a journalism class in my life, but I was excited by the challenge. We hadn't had a newspaper in our school for many years, and no one wanted to fool with it. To everyone's amazement, my initial staff of 10 produced a 12-page, tabloid-sized monthly publication that regularly sold out within 20 minutes.

When you give in too many times, you may gain job security but lose the integrity that will make you a great teacher.

During my second year of teaching the journalism class, I was in a meeting where the principal admitted he had misinformed the student body about the number of absences they could accrue before failing a class. At that time, he admitted he was in violation of school board policy, but to avoid total confusion, he wasn't going to revise his policy until the end of the school year. I saw his point in that it would require a great deal of expense and paperwork to fix the problem in midstream, so I didn't say anything. About a month later, three of my journalism students came to me with the news that two seniors had dropped out of school because of the misinformation. I immediately went to my principal and told him we would be glad to print a clarification in the next issue of the school newspaper to avoid any further confusion. He ordered me to leave the matter alone. I knew he was afraid of losing his job over the issue, but I tried to make him understand that this wrong information was actually causing harm to the students. He told me the newspaper was his and he had every right to censor what we printed. I told him that he needed to assign someone else to produce a public relations sheet for his administration, but I was assigned to help publish a student newspaper. After a heated debate, I recognized he would continue to place his best interests over the students', so I got up to leave. When I reached the door, he asked me if I understood what he expected me to do. I turned around and told him he could always count on me to do the right thing. I knew what was at stake, but we printed the correct information, and the principal never said another word to me about it.

A friend of mine wrote a song in which she described a poet as a "boat rocker in a deep river," and I think that describes me as well. At this point in my life, it would be so much easier to stay in my room and wait for retirement. I've noticed that I don't feel the same fire for the problems that surface year after year—the dress code, the too-complicated record-keeping systems, the scrambling for power. I have a wonderful job and could easily sail through the next few years. But there is always the student who has been denied rights or the good teacher who is ready to quit because of feeling overwhelmed by the system. I've just learned to be a little better at compromise, and I try more often to make sure I have all the facts before I jump in. I have found a few kindred spirits who encourage me, but aren't afraid to tell me when I'm wrong, and I ignore the rest. New teachers are often afraid to stand up for themselves or their students until they have tenure. However, when you give in too many times, you may gain job security but lose the integrity that will make you a great teacher. It's a delicate balance, and the mentors you choose can help you stay on track. The ninth commandment of good teaching? Thou shalt not work in fear; just be sure you're right and that the battle is worth fighting.

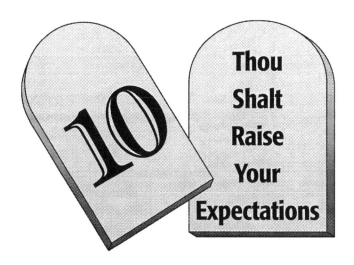

Thou Shalt Raise Your Expectations

One of the biggest mistakes we can make as educators is to view students as empty vessels just waiting for us to remove their lids and pour in the knowledge. Wouldn't it be easy if this were true? But the reality is that the students come to us with all levels of skills, experiences, and expectations. Our challenge is to move them all forward, and this can be an overwhelming task.

I believe in "no excuses" teaching. It may be true that kids these days have become increasingly difficult to teach. The majority come from broken homes; some live in nightmarish conditions; others view school as a total waste of time. Either because of the changes in the evaluation system or because of the unstable conditions in many homes, I find I'm working with more and more students with learning disabilities. I can think of a million reasons to believe these kids are not teachable, but I refuse to do that. This is one area in which I choose to work in ignorance.

When I first started teaching in this small-town high school, a colleague who had lived in the community all her life asked to see my roll sheets. She knew I was new to the area, and she wanted to help me out. She proceeded to call out the names on my roll, letting me know this student was from a good family, that one was bad news, this kid was the mayor's son, that one's daddy was in jail. I was horrified and purposely ignored what she was saying. When the students enter my room at the first of the year, they are all the same to me. I pay no attention to what another teacher has to say about a student's potential. I have a good friend in the counseling office who lets me know about any medical or emotional problems that may affect the students' performances, but other than that, I want to gather my own impressions.

One of the ways I know teachers are headed for burnout is when they begin to offer more and more excuses as to why their students can't be taught. There's always a reason: overcrowded classes, not enough technology, indifferent parents, lack of funds, hostile students, and so on. When your conversation starts sounding similar to this, you need to clearly separate the things you can do something about from the things beyond your control. Teachers rarely accept a student's excuse for being tardy or not turning in homework. They point out that life is not fair and there are no excuses on the job. We teachers are on the job; life is not fair; and we shouldn't make excuses either. We need to fix what we can and get a little more clever about the rest.

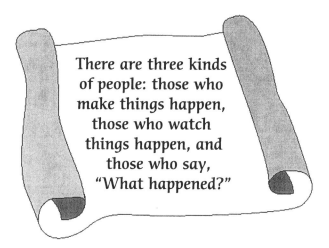

There are three kinds of people: those who make things happen, those who watch things happen, and those who say, "What happened?"

One year, the counseling office put 29 students in my reading lab. I didn't find out until the day before school started. I told the counselors that they had to remove 14 students because the reading lab was designed for a maximum of 15. They said it was a computer mix-up, but the students were already scheduled in, and they'd try to fix it for next semester. I told them they had to make a decision. Did they want me to teach these students to read, or did they want to use me for crowd control? It was up to them. They told me many teachers had overcrowded classes that year and asked me if I thought I was special. I said yes, and luckily they agreed. I also did everything I could to help reduce the class sizes of the other teachers.

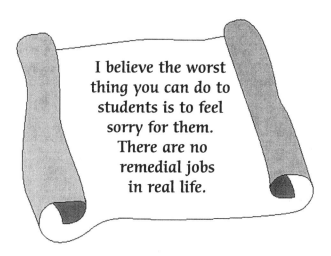

I believe the worst thing you can do to students is to feel sorry for them. There are no remedial jobs in real life.

Another sign in my room says there are three kinds of people: those who make things happen, those who watch things happen, and those who say, "What happened?" I don't believe in being a squeaky wheel to test my power, but I do believe in setting up the best learning atmosphere possible and then doing whatever is necessary to protect it. I begin each class expecting all my students to succeed and I do everything in my power to make sure they do.

In the same manner, I expect a lot out of my students because I believe kids either live up or down to my expectations. I firmly believe a teacher can maintain high standards and still have a very small percentage of failures. I also believe the worst thing you can do to students is to feel sorry for them. There are no remedial jobs in real life. When the kids face the world of work, no one will let them do less than what is required because of pity. There have been times when other people thought I was being mean to certain students by holding them to the same standards as the rest of the class. Robert, a student with Down's syndrome, was placed in my reading lab because he needed to learn to socialize outside his CDC class. He was 16 years old, and few teachers had required him to do much because he had problems controlling his emotions. Usually, they just let Robert sit in the back of the class and do whatever kept him quiet. When I agreed to let him in my reading class, I told his parents I would expect him to work just like my other students. They readily agreed, and I spent some extra time teaching Robert to use the computers and operate in the groups of my class. One day I was called to the office, so I told Robert's group I'd be working with them next and to be ready as soon as I got back. When I returned to the classroom, Robert was on the floor crying and several students were standing helplessly around him. They told me he'd become upset over something and wouldn't get up. I walked over to him, told him it was time to get to work and asked that as long as he was down there, would he mind getting that piece of paper behind that counter? I hadn't been able to reach it myself. Several students looked at me, horrified I had shown so little concern for this special child. Robert glanced up at me, gave a couple more sobs, but quickly retrieved the paper and joined his group at my table. As the semester progressed, he learned to type and mail business letters and work cooperatively in a group. He and his parents were delighted with his success.

Another student who pulled at my heart was in my senior English class. Linda was a little out of her league, but did not want to take a remedial English class. She struggled through most of her assignments but was willing to correct what was wrong. Midway through the year, she woke up one morning to find her mother dead on the sofa. She had no father and one married brother who was not much support. As you can imagine, she missed a number of school days and was overwhelmed when she returned. I did everything in my power to help her catch up, but she continued to miss days because of depression or illness. When I averaged the final grades for her class, we discovered that she had not passed. She burst into tears and begged me to change her grade as many of her other teachers had done. I told her she planned to work as a secretary when she graduated from high school and her writing skills were not even close to what they needed to be. She begged me to think of a way for her to do extra credit work, and I promised I would. When she came to see me the next day, I had a packet of work designed to remediate what she had failed and improve her writing abilities. I told her that most of it needed to be done on the word processor and it had to be completed correctly within one week. Her heart sank when she saw the amount of work, but she took it with her. Later in the day, another teacher told me he'd seen Linda crying in the cafeteria because she had so much to do. I know he thought I was torturing this child who had suffered so much already, but I tried to explain that by just handing her a grade she didn't deserve, I'd be doing her a real disservice. Luckily, Linda rose to the challenge and completed all the necessary work to pass with a D-. I attended graduation mostly for her, and even though it had been a struggle, she was able to proudly claim the diploma she had earned.

You need to constantly raise your expectations for yourself.

I also believe you need to constantly raise your expectations for yourself. After years of refining, I'm finally satisfied with the design of my senior English class, but I would never dream of resting there. Just as my students change every year, what is required of them in the "real world" changes. I have to stay up-to-date with materials and technology or I'll be holding my students back. When I was student teaching, I worked under a teacher who was very generous with his materials. I was flipping through a stack of his files and was dismayed to find the masters to several handouts he reprinted over and over. This teacher had been giving his students the exact same worksheets for 20 years. I'm sure some of it was useful, worthy information, but I would challenge his method for two reasons. One, the sheer volume of facts available to students increases exponentially every year, and what is required of them on the job is in a constant state of flux. Two, one of the quickest roads to burnout is to teach the same thing year after year in the same way. I was terrified when I was assigned the journalism class because it definitely moved me out of my area of expertise. In retrospect, it revitalized me. The easy road is to stay with the familiar. It's much more difficult to become a learner again and scramble to stay ahead of the students, but our energy and enthusiasm will be contagious.

At the beginning of every year, our central office distributes a list of the teachers to be evaluated during that year. This is usually greeted with moans and groans as the teachers anticipate the extra work required. To be honest, I'm not crazy about someone coming into my class to tell me what I'm doing wrong. However, even though I gripe with the best of them, I have never failed to learn something from an evaluation. Sometimes it reinforces my belief in the way I teach. Other times, it makes me question and defend what I'm doing. In either case, it helps me to become a better teacher. I'm not so foolish as to passively accept every suggestion the evaluator may make, but I'm also not so foolish as to think that what I do is perfect and cannot be improved. Even when I think a criticism is dead wrong, it makes me go back and look at my system to see why the observer would interpret it incorrectly. If I think my evaluator just missed the point of what I did, I ignore the critique. If I see the point being made, I incorporate the suggestions into the system.

In the long run, my most useful evaluators are my students. Who better knows the quality of my work? Attached to the final exam for each of my classes is an evaluation sheet. I ask the students to specifically describe the activities we did that were the most and the least useful to them. I also want to know why. I tell them before I hand out the exam that I tear the evaluation sheet off before I grade their tests and I won't look at it until my final grades are on their report cards. I want them to give me honest feedback to help me improve my classes, and buttering me up or putting me down does not affect their grades in any way. I pay very close attention to what my students tell me. Sometimes I'm hurt that a unit I was particularly proud of was more or less meaningless to them. Then again, they surprise me by wanting more of the repetitive work I thought they'd find boring, such as vocabulary and spelling exercises. Whenever I run into former graduates, I ask them to tell me about the things we did in class that turned out to be useful to them later on. I never take a negative evaluation personally; that would be similar to students who throw fits because they receive an F on their tests. An evaluation is nothing more than useful information about someone else's perception of what I'm doing. An evaluation is not what makes a good or bad teacher; it's just another person's opinion. The only people who need to fear evaluations are those who refuse to grow.

In the long run, my most useful evaluators are my students. Who better knows the quality of my work?

A friend of mine has a philosophy that used to drive me nuts, but I've now come to embrace it. He often says, "Just because something is impossible is not a good enough reason not to try." Despite its awkward wording, it holds much truth. We live in the United States, one of the few countries in the world that attempts to educate its entire populace. As teachers, we face an impossible job. We are asked to accept every product, no matter how defective, and get it ready to work. We are asked to be calm, intelligent, loving role models day after day, year after year. We are asked to work through the layers of disuse to find the spark that ignites a student to discover the meaning of his or her life. We are asked to accept the fact that we will never be paid what we're worth, and many of the miracles we perform will go unappreciated. But as I said earlier, if it were easy, anyone could do it. As a teacher, you are part of an elite group of people who can improve the lives of other human beings. The tenth commandment of good teaching? Thou shalt raise your expectations for yourself and your students.

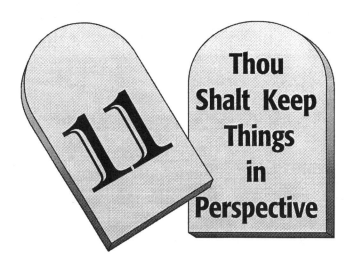

Thou Shalt Keep Things in Perspective

The last year of the century ended like the opening lines of *A Tale of Two Cities;* it was truly the best and the worst of times for me. By October 1999, I was at the top of my game as a teacher. I had received a wall full of awards from my school district and various organizations and was one of six finalists for Tennessee's State Teacher of the Year. My book sales and seminars were going well, and I had a number of articles published in professional journals. I loved my job, and because of my history there, I could get almost anything I wanted done just by making a few phone calls. I had an excellent relationship with my new principal, and many of my coworkers thought of me as a good source of information and guidance. I continued to hear from former students who told me my class was one of their favorites or something I said had changed the direction of their lives. My daughters all lived nearby and were self-supporting, even though two were still in college. Life was good. But by June 2000, my 25-year marriage had ended, I had sold my house, quit my job, and was sitting in a Ryder truck with my brother and all of my worldly goods. I was headed back to California, 2,000 miles away from my children and the life I'd lived for 17 years.

During the last year I lived in Tennessee, I felt like two of the biggest sources of comfort in my life had turned on me—my husband and my students. How could this have happened after all I'd given to them? I covered myself in a cloak of self-pity and railed against such an unfair universe. My marriage was crumbling due to circumstances beyond my control, and every day in 2nd period I had to face the worst class of my teaching career. The ingrates! I wanted an audit from the cosmic forces—the books weren't balancing, and I deserved better than this! For the first time in my life, I began viewing myself as a victim.

I had never written a book about marriage, but I had written one about teaching. The irony did not escape me as I watched a small group of students take control of my class and spin me around like a novice. I knew I was in trouble when I showed the list of students to a colleague and she burst out laughing. "Who did you make mad?" she chuckled. "It looks like they've put every behavior problem in the senior class right in your 2nd period." That wasn't far from the truth; I recognized several of the students' names because they were legends—students who could bring teachers to tears, students whose parents had given several administrators ulcers, students who feared neither failure nor expulsion because they had been diagnosed as having specific learning disabilities or behavior disorders and felt they could not be held accountable for their actions. These students were not at all impressed by me or the honor of being in my class.

I spent what seemed to be too much time walking around feeling sorry for myself. There were days when I was filled with anger over these people who were making my life so miserable. One afternoon I was walking into an optometrist's office when I stepped aside for a man and a woman who were leaving the building. The husband held the door wide for his wife, and I couldn't help but notice that both of her arms had been amputated below the elbows. I felt a little flustered, but she smiled graciously as she and her husband continued joking about the new frames he had chosen. That tiny moment had a huge impact on my life. As I waited for my appointment, I looked in the mirror that lined the walls of the office and said to myself, "You have no problems." Driving home that evening, I realized that even though I was dealing with some stressful circumstances, I'd allowed myself to fall into the trap of blaming my misery on external circumstances against which I was helpless.

Several years ago I wrote a letter to a friend of one of my daughters who was having a difficult time. I told him we view life through a prism. Tilted one way, the lines can seem blurred and distorted, but a slight shift towards the light creates a glorious cascade of colors. After seeing the woman at the eye doctor's, I consciously shifted my perspective from obsessing over my weaknesses to focusing on my strengths. Even though I mourned the end of my marriage, I had been married to a musician for 25 years (which is a miracle in itself), and we had raised three remarkable young women who continue to be a source of great pleasure. And, yes, I was dealing with an unusually difficult group of students, but what a wonderful opportunity to practice what I'd been preaching all these years.

The first thing I did was to stop concentrating on what my students were doing wrong and figure out which of the commandments of good teaching I was breaking. I realized that my two biggest errors were taking my students' inappropriate behaviors personally and not asking for help. The kids didn't know me well enough to hate me, but they had learned to hate authority figures and that was how they saw me. I looked up each of their schedules and talked to their other teachers to find out a little more about their lives outside of my classroom. The vocational teachers and coaches were especially helpful because they knew so much about the students' motivations and their families. Then I made it a point to hang around the cafeteria and in the hallways between classes to talk to the kids informally and find out who their friends were. Instead of seeing the class as one big problem to solve, I looked at them as individuals I needed to get to know. I turned around my relationship with two of the boys because they were best friends with some of my former students. I walked up to the group of them between classes one day and said in mock anger to one of the boys who had loved my class, "Hey, why are you letting Joe treat me so badly?!" Everyone burst out laughing, and we bantered back and forth about Joe's behavior—Joe trying to defend himself and his friends howling over his protests of innocence. This accomplished two things: First, it allowed me to let Joe know about the things that were bothering me in an atmosphere of fun; second, it helped Joe see me as a person his friends liked.

I worked through the class finding allies wherever I could and used my instincts about which approach would be most productive. I'd join some of the students in the cafeteria or library and ask their advice about ways to improve the atmosphere in our class. Another boy did a complete turnaround after I caught his girlfriend and him in an embrace in a back hallway. They expected me to take them to the office, but instead I asked the girlfriend in all earnestness how come Tony was so sweet with her but so sour with me. Tony blushed, but his girlfriend and I had a great talk and she made it a point to stop by my class regularly to ask if his behavior had improved. It had—she was quite a motivator. A few of the kids were more difficult, and I had to make up contracts with their parents and the counselor, but all in all, the atmosphere of the class improved. I hadn't changed the students; I changed the way I responded to the students.

I hadn't changed
the students; I changed
the way I responded
to the students.

Because of my divorce, I had to sell my house and move. One of my nieces, Amy, was teaching at a small school in California and let me know about a job opening there that sounded too good to be true. At first I dismissed the idea—how could I abandon my children and the career I had worked so hard to build? The idea of moving so far away to rebuild my life seemed selfish; this was not the way I'd pictured my life going. Then, one morning I turned on my computer and a quote for the day popped off the screen: "We must be willing to let go of the life we have planned, so as to have the life that is waiting for us."[1] Instead of seeing myself as being shut out of my old life, I started thinking of myself as setting out on another adventure. Recently, one of my daughters won a scholarship that allowed her to go to Japan for an extended period to study ceramics. We were all thrilled she had such an opportunity. We knew we wouldn't see her for a long time, but none of us ever thought of asking her not to go. My daughters have each let me know in no uncertain terms how proud they are of me for having the courage to embrace the life that's waiting for me.

As I write, everything about my life has changed. I've had the pain and the pleasure of feeling like a new teacher as I become acclimated to my new job. In a short time, I've gone from being the lady with all the answers to feeling clueless about what I'm doing, but the scrambling has started a flood of ideas for the new subjects I'll be teaching. My daughters are two time zones away, but we communicate more through e-mail than we did when we lived only a few miles away. Right now I'm filled with gratitude for my past and excited about the future. Special education students know the difference between a handicap and a challenge. Words and attitudes are incredibly powerful, so we have to be careful to choose the ones that give us the most strength. The eleventh commandment of good teaching? When faced with challenges, thou shalt keep things in perspective. The prism is in our hands.

Note

1. This quotation is attributed to Joseph Campbell or E. M. Forster on several Web sites, including the following:

http://www.quoteland.com/quotes/author/163.html (Forster)
http://www.newperspectives.com/free/quotes.html (Campbell)
http://www.ecf.toronto.edu/~suny/mythology.htm (Campbell)

Bibliography

Berne, E. (1961). *Transactional analysis in psychotherapy: A systematic individual and social psychiatry.* New York: Grove Press.

Berne, E. (1964). *Games people play: The psychology of human relationships.* New York: Grove Press.

Ernst, K. (1972). *Games students play (and what to do about them).* Millbrae, CA: Celestial Arts.

Harris, T. A. (1969). *I'm OK, You're OK.* New York: Avon Books.

CORWIN
PRESS